AF505678

ST PAUL'S BIBLIOGRAPHIES
6

A. E. HOUSMAN
A Bibliography

ST PAUL'S BIBLIOGRAPHIES

FORTHCOMING PUBLICATIONS:

A. E. HOUSMAN
A Bibliography

by
JOHN CARTER
and
JOHN SPARROW

Second Edition
Revised by
WILLIAM WHITE

ST PAUL'S BIBLIOGRAPHIES
1982

ST PAUL'S BIBLIOGRAPHIES 6

Originally published in *The Library* in 1940, *A. E. Housman: An Annotated Hand-List* was published in book form by Rupert Hart-Davis in 1952 in the Soho Bibliographies. This second revised and enlarged edition is published under the title of *A. E. Housman: A Bibliography* in 1982 by St Paul's Bibliographies, Foxbury Meadow, Godalming, Surrey.

British Library Cataloguing in Publication Data

Sparrow, John
A. E. Housman – New revised edn.
1. Housman, A. E. – Bibliography
I. Title II. Carter, John, 1905–1976
III. White, William, b. 1910
016.821′912   z8418.6.
ISBN 0-906795-05-2.

© Ernestine Carter and John Sparrow 1952, 1982
© in revisions, William White 1982

Photoset by
Rowland Phototypesetting Ltd, Bury St Edmunds, Suffolk.
Printed in Great Britain by
St Edmundsbury Press, Bury St Edmunds, Suffolk.

CONTENTS

PREFACE TO FIRST EDITION

This hand-list, which now appears in book form for the first time, has been corrected and revised since its original publication in the Transactions of the Bibliographical Society.[1] That it has not been amplified or elaborated is due less to the shortcomings in energy of its compilers than to their knowledge that a full-dress bibliography of Housman is in preparation elsewhere. Since, however, the compilation was designed for the convenience of collectors and amateurs rather than for the instruction of literary critics or scholiasts, we have accepted the suggestion that an unassuming hand-list could still be useful and have therefore maintained the original scope and arrangement.

The arrangement is chronological. The formula of description is elastic: the major pieces being treated more fully than periodical printings, leaflets and the like. The latter are stripped, bibliographically, to the bare essentials, and even in the former we have dispensed with formal collations and title-page transcriptions. Since most of the books are structurally straightforward, we have assumed that the space saved would be more usefully devoted to notes. In these, reference is frequently made to *A. E. Housman, A Sketch, together with a List of his Writings and Indexes to his Classical Papers*, by A. S. F. Gow, Cambridge University Press, 1936 (GOW), and to *A.E.H., Some Poems, Some Letters and a Personal Memoir*, by Laurence Housman, London, Cape, 1937 (MEMOIR): also to Grant Richards's *Housman: 1897–1936*, Oxford University Press, 1941 (RICHARDS) and the *Additions and Corrections* to our original hand-list contributed by Mr. William White to *The Library*[2] (WHITE). The first three of these are essential source-books. The

[1] *The Library*, New Series, Vol. XXI, No. 2, pp. 160–191, 1940.
[2] New Series, Vol. XXIII, No. 1, pp. 31–41.

last gives particulars of the American editions and lists a great number of later periodical printings. It should also be recorded that *A Bibliography of Alfred Edward Housman*, compiled by Theodore G. Ehrsam, M.A., was published in 1941 by the F.W. Faxon Company, of Boston, Mass.

Much of Housman's classical work appeared in the learned journals, and of these *adversaria* and reviews Mr. Gow has provided the definitive list. He is our authority for the attribution to Housman of the anonymous pieces listed under Nos. 13, 17, 20, 22, 23, 30, 34, and 39.[*] He also dealt as fully as need be with letters to the press, obituary notices, miscellaneous (non-classical) reviews, etc., and these have therefore been excluded from the present hand-list. We have not attempted to record those publications, since 1940, in which letters of Housman's, a few recovered stanzas from the poetical note-books[1] and other unpublished trifles have been printed. What, in short, we have tried to do is provide the collector with a reasonably complete guide to Housman's first and other significant editions, and to the first printings of his poems in periodicals or collections.

JOHN CARTER

---

[*] Renumbered in this second edition as Nos. 76, 34, 79, 80, 81, 38, 6, 11.
[1] See Appendix: *A Note on the Poetical MSS.* [Not included in this second edition.]

PREFACE TO REVISED EDITION

Originally published in *The Library*, the Transactions of the Bibliographical Society, New Series, Vol. XXI, pp. 160–191, September 1940, by John Carter and John Sparrow as 'A. E. Housman: an Annotated Check-List', this work appeared, corrected and revised as *A. E. Housman: An Annotated Hand-List* in Rupert Hart-Davis's The Soho Bibliographies II (London, 1952). Now, after almost 30 years, it has been updated, revised, and considerably enlarged, from 49 entries to 140, and the title changed to *A. E. Housman: A Bibliography*, although it should still not be construed as a full-dress descriptive bibliography. What the late John Carter said in his 1952 Preface is still true in 1981: 'the compilation was designed for the convenience of collectors and amateurs rather than for the instruction of literary critics or scholiasts', despite its enlarged scope and rearrangement.

Within the seven headings in the book the arrangement is chronological, and the major pieces by Housman have been treated more fully than periodical writings, leaflets, and the like; indeed, much of the material from the 1952 *Hand-List* has been retained (though numbered differently here), and again formal collations and title-page transcriptions have been dispensed with. Inasmuch as Housman's classical writings in periodicals are listed in A. S. F. Gow's *A. E. Housman: A Sketch, Together with a List of His Classical Papers* (Cambridge: At the University Press, 1936), they have not been repeated here; furthermore, all of the papers themselves were published by the Cambridge University Press in 1972.

Although Housman's reputation as a poet is not what it was in the 1920s or at the time of his death in 1936, articles and books by and about him and his work, such as Richard Perceval Graves's major biography in 1979, continue to be published; and A.E.H.

continues to be collected on both sides of the Atlantic – making this revision of the highly-acclaimed Carter–Sparrow *Hand-List* necessary at this time.

Because the discussion in scholarly publications of Housman's poetical manuscripts has long since ended, I have not retained Mr. Carter's appendix on this subject, interesting as Mr. Carter's writing always was; nor do I include M. Maurice Pollet's 1933 letter from Housman, as that has been reprinted several times and is in Henry Maas's edition of *The Letters of A. E. Housman* (London: Rupert Hart-Davis, 1971). But I do list all the books and journals in which these letters were first printed, as well as A.E.H.'s poems and non-classical prose, for collectors may wish to know where they originally appeared.

As for material about Housman, I have included only those books dealing entirely, or largely, with him and his publications; for the hundreds of articles on Housman and book reviews in magazines and chapters in books – with which I am not here concerned – the reader is referred to my list (though it is not meant to be complete) in *The New Cambridge Bibliography of English Literature*, Vol. 3, 1800–1900, edited by George Watson (Cambridge: At the University Press, 1969), cols. 601–606; to Theodore G. Ehrsam's *A Bibliography of Alfred Edward Housman* (Boston: F. W. Faxon Company, 1941, 44 pp.); to Robert Wooster Stallman's 'Annotated Bibliography of A. E. Housman: A Critical Study', *PMLA*, Vol. LX, pp. 463–502, June 1945; and to B. J. Leggett's *Housman's Land of Lost Content: A Critical Study of 'A Shropshire Lad'* (Knoxville: The University of Tennessee Press, 1970), pp. 139–150. The *Housman Society Journal*, now in its seventh year, is also useful in this respect, especially the bibliographical pieces by Benjamin Franklin Fisher IV.

To repeat, this Housman bibliography deals with all of the scholar-poet's major writings (except for the classical periodical articles and book reviews) and all of the material in books and magazines, and ephemera, that I have been able to find and which, I believe, collectors and those interested in Housman would like to know about. A few books of Housmanania which include nothing original by him and a few books by Housman which reprint material first published elsewhere have also been listed simply as a matter of convenience for readers and Housman enthusiasts. I must emphasize again that the present compilation is by no means a definitive bibliography of A. E. Housman.

Obviously my major debt of gratitude is to the two original compilers, especially to Mr. John Sparrow, who was kind enough to invite me to revise and update *A. E. Housman: An Annotated Hand-List*; and for their help, I must thank Mr. David McKitterick, of the Cambridge University Library, and Mr. Robert Cross, of the British Museum (Natural History) and St Paul's Bibliographies.

WILLIAM WHITE

Franklin Village, Michigan, USA
20 July 1981

ILLUSTRATIONS

SUMMARY LIST

BOOKS AND PAMPHLETS

CONTRIBUTIONS TO BOOKS

BIOGRAPHIES, ETC., SOME CONTAINING ORIGINAL MATERIAL

CONTRIBUTIONS TO PERIODICALS

PERIODICALS CONTAINING
ORIGINAL MATERIAL

BOOKS AND PAMPHLETS ABOUT A.E.H.

TRANSLATIONS

BOOKS & PAMPHLETS

I

INTRODUCTORY LECTURE
(1892)

Introductory Lecture delivered before the Faculties of Arts and Laws and of Science in University College, London, October 3, 1892 . . . *Nescit vox missa reverti.* Cambridge: Printed at the University Press, 1892.

215 × 135 mm. Stitched, without wrappers. 10 leaves.

'This was not Housman's inaugural lecture as professor but an annual lecture introductory to the session, the delivery of which, in 1892, fell to him as junior professor. Its theme is that learning, literary and scientific alike, is desirable for its own sake.' (Gow, p. 75.)

The *Lecture* was printed for distribution to the members of the Faculties before whom it was delivered. It was not published or for sale at the time, and less than a score of copies seem to have survived.

See Plate I.

Ia

Cambridge: Printed at the University Press, 1933.

220 × 140 mm. Blue wrappers, printed in black. 14 leaves.

This private reprint contains a prefatory note; but except for a correction made by the author in the quotation from King George III on p. 16, the text itself is reprinted without alteration.

I

INTRODUCTORY LECTURE

DELIVERED BEFORE

THE FACULTIES OF ARTS AND LAWS AND OF SCIENCE

IN

UNIVERSITY COLLEGE, LONDON,

OCTOBER 3, 1892,

BY

A. E. HOUSMAN, M.A.,

PROFESSOR OF LATIN.

Nescit vox missa reverti.

CAMBRIDGE:

PRINTED AT THE UNIVERSITY PRESS.

1892

I.   Title-page of No. 1.
From a copy trimmed 5 mm. at the top.

100 copies were printed for John Carter and John Sparrow. 25 were reserved for the author. None was for sale. Two copies were printed on blue paper.

Of the suggestion for this reprint Housman wrote 9 November 1933: 'Although I was not a willing party to the original publication of my introductory lecture at University College, published it is, and your flattering proposal, if carried out, will not make matters perceptibly worse; so I offer no objection, and indeed I should be glad of a few additional copies.' And on 5 December: 'I should like to have it stated that the Council of University College, not I, had the lecture printed. I consented, because it seemed churlish to refuse. This is the purport of *Nescit vox missa reverti*.'

1b

Cambridge: At the University Press, 1937.

183 × 123 mm. Blue boards, printed in black. 24 leaves (the first and last blank).

This is the first published edition. The text, which follows that of 1a, is preceded by a *Note* by A. S. F. Gow.

1c

New York: The Macmillan Company; Cambridge: At the University Press, 1937.

182 × 129 mm. Blue cloth, lettered in gilt on spine (vertically) and front cover. 24 leaves (the first and last blank).

This is the first American edition. The text and A. S. F. Gow's *Note* follow 1b. The pagination and page size differ.

II.   Variant labels of No. 2.

2

A SHROPSHIRE LAD
(1896)

A Shropshire Lad. London: Kegan Paul, Trench, Trubner & Co. Ltd., MDCCCXCVI.

172 × 110 mm. 52 leaves. Pale blue paper boards, white parchment back, cream paper label lettered vertically in red. The title-page is printed in red and black.

Accompanying the copy given by A. E. H. to Mr. Gow (mentioned below) was a note, reading: 'I am afraid that you will despise not only the print and paper, for which I am not responsible, but also the binding and title-page, for which I am.'

There was no printed dust-jacket, but Messrs. Kegan Paul's records show a charge of ninepence for 'papering'. This would accord with the glazed paper jackets which have survived on some copies. The book was published, probably during the first week of March, at half a crown.

Of this first edition 500 copies were printed, of which 150 (ready bound) were exported for publication in New York by John Lane. These were furnished with a cancel title-page bearing the Lane imprint and dated 1897.

The title
The volume was originally called *Poems by Terence Hearsay*. This title was exchanged for the final one at the suggestion of Professor A. W. Pollard. The book was offered to Macmillan,[1] but declined; and it was subsequently printed at the author's expense for publication by Messrs. Kegan Paul.

The paper label
There are four variants of the printed paper label, all of which are shown in Plate II, and while it is fairly certain that the one marked A is the primary, the circumstances surrounding the production of

---

[1] Also to three other publishers, according to Mr. Percy Withers, one of them being A. H. Bullen (*A Buried Life*, p. 68).

5

B remain obscure. Evidence for the priority of A is provided by the copyright examples in the British Museum (received 17 April 1896) and in Bodley (U.L.C. copy has been missing for some years); by one of the 'author's copies' which Housman in later years presented to Mr. Gow; by the copies given on publication to his sister Mrs. Symons, and his friend A. W. Pollard, all of which are A. This is not proof. For even such a concatenation of support for A would be invalidated by the discovery of copies with the B label bearing inscriptions contemporary with publication. But we have seen none such; and since the variants seem to us certainly successive, not simultaneous, the evidence at present suggests that B must be later.

The immediately obvious hypotheses,

(1) That A was used for the English, B for the American copies,
(2) That A was used for the first English binding-up (250) and the American issue (150); B for the second English binding-up (100),

are at once ruled out by the inconvenient fact that the two variants are found impartially in conjunction with both London and New York title-pages. Yet Messrs. Kegan Paul's records contain only the single entry, for 'a printing of 500 back labels in red ink'. And we are accordingly reduced to the supposition that at some time before the casing of the New York consignment some portion of this 500 was either spoiled or mislaid at the bindery, and replaced by a second printing which was thereafter used indiscriminately with the remainder of the first.

It is tempting to hazard the further conjecture, that the loss or damage occurred between the completion of the first binding-up (of the English issue) and the binding-up of the American issue. This would give
(1) first English binding—all A labels
(2) American issue—A and B labels, mixed
(3) second English binding—A and B labels, mixed; or, possibly, all B labels. This would mean that, of copies of the first (English) edition, A-labelled copies may be of either binding, while B-labelled copies must be of the second. But this remains a second degree conjecture.

David A. Randall, in *The Book Collector* (Vol. 22, p. 176, Summer 1973), reported that the Lilly Library, Indiana University, had—in addition to the A and B labels—two variants which he labelled C and D, which have the rounded O and U, as contrasted with A and B; further the D label is printed in purple, not red, ink, and with a full stop after Housman's name. (See the accompanying plate, showing all four *Shropshire Lad* variant labels.)

A slip case?
The copy presented by A.E.H. to Mr. Gow, and now in Cambridge University Library, presents a problem which we have been unable to solve: for it is in a maroon board slip-case. Now, although the gift was made only in 1935, this copy had been unearthed from among Housman's papers and was understood to have been one of those sent him on publication. It was unopened, in its glazed jacket, and had clearly been long preserved in the slip-case, which indeed has every appearance of being original. Mr. Gow wrote: 'When Housman gave me my copy I said I had not known it had been published in a slip-case and he said that it had . . . he did not tell me any more.'

But before accepting the evidence of our own eyes and of the author's recollection, and stating that *A Shropshire Lad* was issued in a slip case, we must consider the following points:
(1) There is no record of such a thing in Messrs. Kegan Paul's ledgers; and their meticulous accounting for the expenses of a 'commission' book is evidenced by the ninepenny entry for wrapping paper.
(2) Mr. Laurence Housman is positive, and so was Professor Pollard (who received a presentation copy on publication) that the book had no slip case; while Mrs. Symons wrote: 'I am practically certain that none of the copies of *A Shropshire Lad* came to any of us in slip cases. Alfred sent all of us copies, three of which came into my possession. Both my step-mother and I were great hoarders and I am sure we should have kept such covers.'
(3) No other example of it is recorded.
The last point does not carry much weight. But the others are difficult to explain; and the evidence of the contemporary presentation copies rules out the hypothesis that slip-cases were specially provided for the author's complimentary copies. The choice, then, seems to lie between regarding Mr. Gow's slip-cased copy as unique, and inferring from it that others must have been so issued.

Later editions
The second edition (8vo, green buckram, 500 copies; now a scarce book) was published by Grant Richards in 1898. 'It contains nothing new,' wrote Housman once, 'except a few misprints', and some of these he corrected in his own copy. With a few exceptions (e.g. Riccardi Press 1914, Alcuin Press 1929, Harrap 1940), Grant Richards and (since 1927) his successor firm, the Richards Press, have published all subsequent English editions of *A Shropshire Lad*.[1] The book was reprinted in 1900, 18mo, 'Smaller Classics' series (1,000 copies, now very scarce); 1903 f'cap 8vo, red wrappers, 2,000 copies; the remaining sheets reissued (red buckram) in 1906 with cancel title. In 1907 it was included in the publisher's 'Omar' series, royal 32mo, at 6*d.* in cloth and 1*s.* in leather (5,000 copies printed); and in the same year an edition (500) on hand-made paper was put out in green buckram.

In 1908 appeared the first illustrated edition (2,000 copies), a large 8vo, in cream cloth at 6*s* or limp leather at 7*s.* 6*d.* There are eight plates, reproduced in colour from water colours by William Hyde depicting Shropshire landscapes. A scarce 32mo edition of the same year has one of these illustrations reproduced in monochrome as a frontispiece. A set of decorations was designed by Lovat Fraser in 1920, but Housman did not like them and they were never used. They were, however, reproduced some years afterwards under the title *Sixty-three Unpublished Designs*, with an introduction by Holbrook Jackson explaining their relation to *A Shropshire Lad*, in a booklet issued by the First Edition Club.

The Text
The text remained unchanged, except for misprints, till 1922, when the author made two alterations:—

[1] In the 1960s, although printings continued to be made from older plates, the dust wrappers read, under the line 'The Richards Press Ltd': 'Martin Secker: Director'. The spine also had the words, 'John Baker', and later the wrapper read, 'London: Published by John Baker for The Richards Press, 5 Royal Opera Arcade, Pall Mall'. After John Baker's death in 1968, his list was taken over by the Garnstone Press. A 1975 printing of *A Shropshire Lad* has the Garnstone Press imprint on the title page. The edition printed by Harrap, with wood engravings by Agnes Miller Parker, went through 13 impressions from 1940 to 1981.

In XXXVIII, 10   *Thick on the wind are sown* becomes
                  Loose on the wind are sown
In LII, 9   *He hears: long since forgotten* becomes
             He hears: no more remembered

That an author so impatient of inaccuracy ('accuracy is a duty, not a virtue,' he wrote in 1927) should have put up for many years with a publisher so negligent, is testimony to Housman's warm personal regard for Grant Richards. Of the second edition—the first from his new publisher—he recalled in 1935 that no proofs were sent for his correction, and he wrote after its publication (Richards, p. 26) 'last time someone played games with the punctuation.' Of the third edition he was able to say (Richards, p. 48) that it was 'almost exactly correct,' and he corrected proofs of subsequent reprints in 1902 and 1904. In 1914, however, he had to remind Richards that he had seen no proofs of the 1912 edition, and four years later he noticed eight mistakes in the current 8vo edition, 'probably all taken over from 1916.' In 1922 he wrote of the 1918 and 1921 editions: 'in both I find the same set of blunders in punctuation and ordering of lines, some of which I have corrected again and again' (Richards, p. 201). Proofs of the impending reprint were accordingly sent to him and returned corrected in October; but in December he writes (Richards, p. 206): 'In the copies of the small Shropshire Lad which you sent me a few weeks ago, the corrections I gave you have not been made.' In 1927 he notes 'a disgusting misprint' in the 1925 reprint, and in the following year (Richards, p. 244) he writes: 'At the present moment my feelings towards you are much embittered by the discovery that your last small edition of *A Shropshire Lad* contains 15 errors, some of them filthy.' He marked these (and indeed half a dozen more) in his copy of the 1926 printing (32mo), which survives, and asterisked the five most important ones, from which an errata slip was prepared for insertion in the remaining copies. This is the only errata slip we have noticed in any edition of *A Shropshire Lad*.

American editions
These were numerous and, until 1922, mostly unauthorised, for the book was not protected by copyright. For particulars, see William White, *The Library*, Fourth Series, Vol. XXIII, pp. 33–34, June

1942: and Fifth Series, Vol. VII, pp. 202–204, September 1952,[2] and the appendix to Carl J. Weber's 'Jubilee Edition' (Waterville, Maine, 1946).

[2] After the New York: John Lane, 1897 edition (from the English plates) there were other John Lane printings from 1906 to 1920; Dodd, Mead & Company (New York) reprinted these editions (unauthorised) with new title page in 1925 and its own edition in 1931. Other unauthorised American editions include: Philadelphia: Henry Altemus Company [1902] in several formats; Portland, Maine: Thomas B. Mosher, 1906, 1913, 1922; New York: Mitchell Kennerley, 1906, 1914 (from Grant Richards's sheets); Girard, Kansas: Haldeman-Julius Company, [1920], 1931; Boston: The Four Seas Company, 1919 (reprinted by Bruce Humphries, 1931; International Pocket Library, 1936); New York: Illustrated Editions Company, 1932 (these sheets were reissued by Grosset & Dunlap, Three Sirens Press, Concord Books, Hartsdale House, Halcyon House, Arden Book Company, Deluxe Editions, and other imprints with various bindings); New Rochelle, New York (later Mt. Vernon): Peter Pauper Press, 1934, 1936, 1942, 1944, 1945, 1948 (and continuing to 1981, same plates, differing colored ink, bindings, dust-wrappers); New York: The Heritage Press, 1935 (reissued by The Heritage Club, 1938, 1951—with an appendix of bibliographical material by Carl J. Weber); Philadelphia: David McKay Company, 1935; Cleveland, Ohio, and New York: World Publishing Company, 1942 (new edition, 1947); Waterville, Maine: Colby College Library (Jubilee Edition, with notes and a Bibliography by Carl J. Weber, 1946 (new edition, 1946, reprinted by Greenwood Press, New York, 1980); New York: Thomas Y. Crowell Company, 1946; Mount Vernon, New York: Golden Eagle Press, 1946 (new edition, 1958?); New York: Hartsdale House, 1947; Chicago: Wilson & Follett Co., 1948?; Garden City, New York: Garden City Publishing Co., 1950?; New York: R. H. Macy & Co., Inc., n.d.; Toronto: Ambassador Books, n.d. (1948?); New York: Somerset Books, Inc., n.d. (1950?); New York: Shakespeare House, 1951; New York: Avon Books, 1950 (Supplementary Material by Joseph Mersand, Avon Library Edition, Sixth Printing, 1966; reprinted, Bard Books, 1972); New York: The Greystone Press, Castle Books, 1951; New York: Franklin Watts, Inc., 1968; Boston, Mass.: Brandon Press, Inc., 1980.

The authorised American edition was issued by Henry Holt and Company, New York, in 1922 from Grant Richards sheets, and the same year from their own sheets. There have been various editions in cloth and leather and Holt had printed 25,060 copies of *A Shropshire Lad* through 1940; reprints appeared in 1942, 1944 (twice), and in a new edition in 1946; by 1960, when the firm became Holt, Rinehart and Winston, they ceased to publish *A Shropshire Lad* separately from *The Collected Poems*.

3

MANILII ASTRONOMICA

(1903–1930)

M. Manilii Astronomicon Liber Primus recensuit et enarravit A. E. Housman . . . Londinii apud Grant Richards MDCCCCIII.

215 × 141 mm. Dull blue boards, printed in black, dark blue linen spine, white label, edges cut flush.

On p. v is the dedication to Moses Jackson, 28 lines of Latin elegiacs. Pp. vii–lxxv contain the famous preface.

The paper label to Vol. 1 is found in two forms:
  (*a*) MANILIVS. HOVSMAN
  (*b*) MANILII I. HOVSMAN
Although the publishers have no record or recollection of the change, it must be supposed that the more precise form is the later. It would be reasonable to guess that *b* was substituted for *a* (of which the compilers have seen only one copy in twenty years) when it became necessary to differentiate Book I from the editions of the later books which were published subsequently; for Mr. Gow stated on Housman's own authority (*Times Literary Supplement*, 6 February 1937, p. 19) that when he published his edition of Book I he had not yet decided to proceed with an edition of the whole poem.[1] Yet at least three *a* copies known to us were demonstrably issued before June 1903.

There are minor variations in label (*b*) and also in the labelling of the later volumes (see Richards, pp. 170, 180). Presumably fresh batches of labels were printed as required for successive binding orders.

The succeeding volumes were issued by the same publishing firm[2] in uniform style. Book II (1912) contains an astrological excursus by way of preface, as do Books III (1916) and IV (1920). In Book V

---

[1] Pp. 82–99 of Vol. 1 contain emendations of Books II–IV (those to Book V had been published in *Journal of Philology*).

[2] In Book V this had become 'apud Societatem *The Richards Press*'.

11

(1930) besides some *Addenda* to the preceding volumes at the end, the particular preface to the contents is preceded (pp. v–xxxvii) by a general retrospective survey of Manilian studies during the intervening 27 years. In its opening paragraph Housman gives the following particulars of the publication of the five volumes:

'All were produced at my own expense and offered to the public at much less than cost price;[1] but this unscrupulous artifice did not overcome the natural disrelish of mankind for the combination of a tedious author with an odious editor. Of each volume there were printed 400 copies: only the first is yet sold out,[2] and that took 23 years; and the reason why it took no longer is that it found purchasers among the unlearned, who had heard that it contained a scurrilous preface and hoped to extract from it a low enjoyment.'

An *editio altera* was published in 1937 by the Cambridge University Press. It was reproduced by photolithography from the original edition, with various corrections, omissions and rearrangements. Each volume has an introductory note by A. S. F. Gow.

The five volumes were reprinted by photolithography in two volumes in 1972: MARCUS MANILIUS | ASTRONOMICON | I [II] |. RECENSUIT ET ENARRAVIT | ALFRED EDWARD HOUSMAN | QUINQUE TOMI IN DUOBUS TOMIBUS | 1972 | GEORG OLMS VERLAG | HILDESHEIM · NEW YORK | (publisher's device) | . Printed in Germany, bound in blue cloth, lettered in gilt on the front cover and spine. They do not contain Gow's introductions.

3a

An *editio minor*, in one volume, was published in 1932 by the Cambridge University Press.

---

[1] Books I–III, 4*s*. 6*d*. each; Book IV, 6*s*; Book V, 7*s*. 6*d*. The formidable bulk and complexity of the *apparatus criticus* must have been very expensive to set up. Book I was printed by R. & R. Clark, the remainder by Maclehose.

[2] Book II eventually sold out also. The remaining stock of the succeeding volumes was pulped.

4
IVVENALIS SATVRAE
(1905)

D. Iunii Iuuenalis Saturae editorum in usum edidit A. E. Housman. Londinii apud E. Grant Richards. MDCCCCV.

214 × 141 mm. Apricot coloured boards, printed in black, linen black, white paper label, edges cut flush.

Preface, pp. v–xxxvi.

Printed by R. & R. Clark and published at 4s. 6d.

In 1903 Housman had been asked by J. P. Postgate to undertake the recension of Juvenal for the *Corpus Poetarum Latinorum* (see No. 36) for which he had already edited Ovid's *Ibis* (Vol. I, 1894, with a short note on the MSS, in Latin, p. xxi). (See No. 31.) This text of Juvenal (Vol. II, pt. V, 1905) was again prefaced (pp. viii, ix) by a short Latin note on the MSS. Of the independent, and much fuller, edition here described he wrote, at the end of the preface: 'it is an enterprise undertaken in haste and in humane concern for the relief of a people sitting in darkness.'

4a

Second edition, Cambridge University Press, 1931.

With minor corrections and an additional preface occupying pp. xxxvii–lvii; reprinted (by photolithography) 1938.

5
LAST POEMS
(1922)

Last Poems. London: Grant Richards Ltd., MDCCCCXXII.

183 × 123 mm. 40 leaves. Dark blue buckram, gilt tops, lettered in gilt on the spine and front cover. Issued in a dust jacket of white surfaced paper, printed in black. Of the first impression 4,000 copies were printed. Published 19 October.

The text is preceded by a prefatory note, in the course of which Housman writes: 'it is best that what I have written should be printed while I am here to see it through the press and control its spelling and punctuation.' Against this sentence in his own copy he pencilled 'Vain hope!' with a direction to p. 52, where he had inserted the final punctuation marks missing from the first two lines. When the publisher's attention was called to this blemish he offered to insert an errata slip in the remaining copies: but Housman replied on a post-card: 'No, don't put in an errata slip. The blunder will probably enhance the value of the 1st edition in the eyes of bibliophiles, an idiotic class.' The stops were replaced in the second impression (before 26 October).

Published in America by Henry Holt and Company, New York, in 1922. There were numerous reprints.

Of the poems in this volume, the following had been previously printed:

> II. 'As I gird on for fighting'. See No. 85.
>
> The only textual change is in stanza 2, line 1, where *In dust the round world over* now reads *Think I, the round.*
>
> III. 'Her strong enchantments failing'. See No. 83.
>
> The title there used has now been dropped. Two drafts (besides the fair copy and the cancelled proof of 1895) survive, from which it is clear that the *Edwardian* (1915) printing represents, even allowing for possible errors in copying, a transitional state of the text. It has *broken* for *failing* in line 1; *poison* for *poisons*, line 3; *his foot on* for *the knife at*, line 4: and there are half a dozen variations of pointing.
>
> IV. *Ilic Jacet* ('Oh hard is the bed they have made him'). See No. 77.
>
> The *Edwardian* (1915) text shows two verbal variations (*That* for *And*, line 8, and *love that* for *sweetheart*, line 16) and is more heavily punctuated, especially in stanza 2. The *Academy* (1900) text shows three (*blankets*, line 2,

bedside for *chamber*, line 9, *Oh thin is the quilt* for *And low is the roof*, line 13), all of which are found in a surviving early draft of the poem; but its punctuation is lighter.

XVII. *Astronomy* ('The Wain upon the northern steep'). See No. 35.

XXV. *The Oracles* (''Tis mute, the word they went to hear'). See No. 33.

Apart from the two misprints noted under No. 33, there are five differences of punctuation between the two texts (*Last Poems* being the heavier in each case) and one trivial verbal change (*O* for *Oh*, line 9).

XXXIV. *The First of May* ('The orchards half the way'). See No. 82.

In stanza 2, line 4, the final comma has been changed to a semi-colon; and in stanza 3, line 4, *stands lofty on the dead*, is altered to *stands planted*.

XXXVII. *Epitaph on an Army of Mercenaries* ('These, in the day when heaven was falling'). See No. 86.

XXXVIII. 'Oh stay at home, my lad, and plough.' See No. 39.

Included in *A Tribute to Thomas Hardy O.M. June 2 1919* (1919), a MS volume.

The title *Revolution* was first given by the author to XXXVI when he gave permission for its inclusion in a Winchester College 'Lines Book' in 1926.

6

Address of Condolence on the Death of Queen Alexandra

(1925)

413 × 271 mm. Broadsheet, one leaf, verso blank. Printed (on 2 December) in red and black at the Cambridge University Press. No imprint. The Address, headed by the University Arms, begins 'To the King's Most Excellent Majesty' &c.; and is dated 28 November 1925.

Two copies were printed on vellum and two on paper. One vellum copy, with the official seal, and one paper copy were sent to the King. The other paper copy is preserved in the University Registry.

The Address was reprinted (and first published) in the *Cambridge University Reporter* of 22 December 1925 (p. 442) under the title of 'Address of Condolence to His Majesty the King on the death of Her Majesty the Queen Mother'. Housman's authorship has probably never been officially divulged.

7

LVCANI BELLVM CIVILE

(1926)

M. Annaei Lucani Belli Ciuilis Libri Decem. Editorum in usum edidit A. E. Housman. Oxonii apud Basilium Blackwell MDCCCCXXVI.

215 × 138 mm. Dark blue cloth, gilt lettered on the spine.

Issued in a grey dust-jacket, printed in black.

Preface pp. [v]–xxxv. There is no printer's imprint. Published at 12*s.* 6*d.* in January 1926.

In December Housman wrote to Mr. Percy Withers that the book 'sells just twice as fast as *A Shropshire Lad* did' (*A Buried Life*, p. 76).

Second edition, with corrections, March 1927, and (third impression) in April 1950.

Published in America by Harvard University Press, Cambridge, Massachusetts.

8
A Fragment
(1930)

A Fragment preserved by oral tradition and said to have been composed by A. E. Housman in a dream. 1930.

173 × 139 mm. 2 leaves, folded. 37 copies printed (by Unwin Brothers, Woking) for John Carter and John Sparrow. There is no imprint.

This unauthorized leaflet contains the four-line stanza *The bells jostle in the tower*, of which a more correct text was afterwards given in the *Memoir* (No. IX). It was privately circulated as a Christmas card.

Collected Poems, p. 224.

9

THE NAME AND NATURE OF POETRY
(1933)

The Name and Nature of Poetry. Cambridge: At the University Press, 1933.

184 × 123 mm. Pinkish buff paper boards, printed in black.

This, the Leslie Stephen Lecture, was delivered at Cambridge on 9 May 1933 (the 22nd anniversary of Housman's Inaugural). The first impression (3,000 copies) contained a misquotation from Shakespeare on p. 41, which Housman corrected in his own copy, but which persisted through at least two reprints.

Reprinted numerous times in England, by Cambridge University Press and (in 1939) by the Readers' Union, London, for its members.

The American edition, published by The Macmillan Company, New York (with its name and that of Cambridge University Press on the title page), was published in 1933; after nine reprintings the Macmillan agency was terminated and reprintings after 1950 contained only the imprint of Cambridge University Press. (See White, *The Library*, Fifth Series, Vol. VII, p. 204.) The error on p. 40 of the American edition was never corrected.

10

THREE POEMS

(1935)

Three Poems: The Parallelogram. The Amphisbaena. The Crocodile. . . . Privately Printed in the Department of English at University College, London. MCMXXXV.

216 × 165 mm. Blue wrappers, printed in black. 8 leaves.

The three facetious pieces (Nos. 79, 80, 81) were collected, with the author's permission, by Geoffrey Tillotson: see his 'The Publication of A. E. Housman's Comic Poems,' *English* (Magazine of the English Association, London), Vol. I, No. 6, pp. 485–493, 1937.

There are three slight errors: the third line on p. 8 should begin a new paragraph; 'advancing' (p. 6, line 2) has a figure one instead of an 'i'; and in some copies a few letters at the bottom of p. 5 did not print—these letters, 'c[lear]' and 'r[ear]', were supplied in pen and ink.

An American printing, for private distribution, was produced as *The Parallelogram, The Amphisbaena, The Crocodile* by Jake Zeitlin (printed by Grant Dahlstrom) in Los Angeles in 1941, in light buff wrappers, 160 × 117 mm, 8 leaves. The text follows No. 10, above, and contains four misprints: p. 1, line 7, comma missing after 'out'; p. 7, line 11, comma missing at end; p. 8, line 2, should begin a new paragraph; p. 9, line 5, should read 'hills' for 'hill'.

11
Jubilee Address to King George V
(1935)

383 × 274 mm. 2 leaves folded, printed in red and black. There is no title.

Opening with the University Arms, the text begins: 'To the King's Most Excellent Majesty May it Please Your Majesty We, the Chancellor, Masters, and Scholars of the University of Cambridge, desire to approach You with our loyal and dutiful congratulations on the completion of the twenty-fifth year of Your Majesty's reign'. The fourth page is blank, and there is no imprint.

2 copies were printed on vellum and 24 on paper by the University Press on 29 April.

The Address was reprinted (and first published) in the *Cambridge University Reporter* of 14 May 1935, under the title 'Address to His Majesty the King'. Housman's authorship has probably never been officially divulged; but for the benefit of those collectors who relish the unattainable trifle it may be added that the first printing of any part of the Address over his name is believed to have been the Latin Prose Composition paper for the Sixth Classical at Charterhouse, dated July 1935 but actually printed in May.

Reprinted, with variants and only in part, in Laurence Housman's *AEH* (see No. 52, pp. 107–108).

12
For my funeral
(1936)

Trinity College. Alfred Edward Housman, Fellow . . . 4 May 1936, &c.

This leaflet (177 × 115 mm.) of two leaves folded carries the order of service for the funeral on the first page; the second and fourth are blank; on the third are printed for the first time the three stanzas beginning 'O thou that from thy mansion', signed in full, with the note (from the MS.) 'Melody by Melchior Vulpius. Harmonised by J. S. Bach'. There is no imprint.

300 copies were printed by the Cambridge University Press for the funeral. Line 7 of p. [1] has a misprint, *Ecclesiasticus* for *Ecclesiastes*. Between 4 May and 8 May a further 100 were printed, with the misprint corrected and a slenderer initial capital for the poem itself. (See Plate III.) The hymn was sung at the funeral, to the tune of No. 232 in the *English Hymnal*.

The poem was first published in *The Evening Standard* of 4 May (p. 3) under the title, *For my funeral*, which was afterwards used in *More Poems* XLVII.

First published in America in an article, 'Housman's Own Hymn Is Sung at His Burial', *New York Herald Tribune*, 5 May 1936 (p. 1).

Mr. Gow writes: 'The title was Housman's, but I suppose he meant it rather as a direction than as a title. The piece was given to the Dean in a sealed envelope to keep until wanted.'

Mr. Laurence Housman states that, in a fair copy preserved in the family, A. E. H. added: 'Tune, Brief Life is here our portion'; and also the following footnote to the three stanzas: '(To which the choir, unless forcibly restrained, will add:

All glory to the Father
All glory to the Son
All glory to the Spirit
While endless ages run).'

He then subjoined the further note: 'The printer will already have altered *place* to *space*.'

Though the printer did not make this particular mistake, there was indeed a misprint in the Order of Service for the funeral, as noted above. It was appropriately ironical that misprints should have pursued Housman to the grave: even in the *Deaths* column of *The Times* his age was given as 76 instead of 77.

TRINITY COLLEGE

ALFRED EDWARD HOUSMAN

FELLOW

Kennedy Professor of Latin

4 MAY 1936

PSALM CXXXIX. *Domine, probasti.*

LESSON. *Ecclesiasticus* XI, 7—XII, 7.

HYMN. O thou that from thy mansion.

Nunc dimittis.

ob. 30 April 1936

aet. LXXVII

O thou that from thy mansion
  Through time and place to roam,
 Dost send abroad thy children,
 And then dost call them home,

That men and tribes and nations
  And all thy hand hath made
May shelter them from sunshine
  In thine eternal shade :

We now to peace and darkness
  And earth and thee restore
Thy creature that thou madest
  And wilt cast forth no more.

A. E. HOUSMAN
Melody by Melchior Vulpius,
Harmonized by J. S. Bach

III. The two printings of No. 12.

13
MORE POEMS
(1936)

More Poems. London: Jonathan Cape (1936).

200 × approximately 145 mm. 36 leaves, plus frontispiece reproduction of the portrait drawing by Francis Dodd. Dark blue
buckram, lettered in gilt on spine and front cover. Issued in a
blue-grey dust-jacket, printed in red and black.

The text is preceded by a preface signed 'L.H.' (Laurence Housman),
and at the end is a list of *Dated Poems*, drawn from the author's
note-books.

The poems in his posthumous volume were all printed here for the
first time except the following:

IV. *The Sage to the Young Man* ('O youth whose heart is
right'). The text here differs in half a dozen particulars
from that of *The Edwardian*, 1916; but the authority of the
latter is dubious (see note to No. 84).

V. *Diffugere Nives* ('The snows are fled away, leaves on the
shaws'). See No. 32. There are five differences in punctuation between the two texts.[1]

XLVII. *For my funeral* ('O thou that from thy mansion'). See
No. 12.

XLVIII. *Alta Quies* ('Good-night. Ensured release'). See No. 69.
The title and lines 4 and 5 differ completely from the
earlier text.[1]

More Poems was published on 26 October. The first impression of
8,856 copies is indistinguishable from the second (5,081 copies),
which was called for before publication. In the third impression
(7,500 copies) which is described on the verso of the title as
'second', misprints were corrected on pp. 26, 62, 67 and a deletion
was made in the list of dated poems (p. 71)—'Morning up the

---

[1] The earlier text was restored in *The Collected Poems* (see No. 14).

eastern stair' having been included in the list although as yet unpublished. A further misprint (on p. 32) was corrected in the following impression.

A special impression was printed on hand-made paper, with gilt tops, and cased in rust-coloured linen with matching leather back. 227 × 147 mm. It was limited to 379 copies and published on the same day as the trade edition. It contains an extra illustration facing p. 32: a reproduction of the original manuscript of the poem opposite, 'Tarry, delight'.

The American edition (New York: Alfred A. Knopf) was published the same day as the English. Mr. White records (*The Library*, Fourth series, Vol. XXIII, p. 36) that, in addition to minor differences in the Preface, there are as many as 63 variations in the text of the poems themselves.

14

THE COLLECTED POEMS
(1939)

The Collected Poems. London: Jonathan Cape (1939).

200 × 140 mm. 128 leaves. Dark blue cloth, lettered in gilt on the spine. Issued in a blue-grey dust-jacket printed in red and black.

The *Contents* leaf ([A]3) was cancelled before publication, in order to incorporate the acknowledgements to The Richards Press for *A Shropshire Lad* and *Last Poems*.

This volume contains all the poems in *A Shropshire Lad, Last Poems* (but not the prefatory note), and *More Poems*: the eighteen poems previously printed on pp. 214–221 of Laurence Housman's *A.E.H.*: one poem printed for the first time (No. XX of the section *Additional Poems*): one poem (*Additional Poems* XIX) previously but posthumously printed in *The Virginia Quarterly Review*, 1939: and finally three poems and three translations here first collected— Nos. 29, 69, 75, 78. At the end of the book are a *Note on the Text* by its then anonymous editor (John Carter), an *Index of First Lines*, and an *Index of Titled Poems*. The editor had access to the manuscripts from which *More Poems* and the poems printed in the *Memoir* had been printed, where these survived; and in some places further scrutiny made it possible to present a more correct text. The original text of Nos. 32 and 69 in this hand-list was restored: Nos. 29, 70, and 75, were reprinted without alteration: No. 78 was printed from a manuscript copy, and shows minor variations from the 1902 text.

Housman wrote to a correspondent in 1934 that *A Shropshire Lad* and *Last Poems* 'will never be joined together while I am here to prevent it, and I think it a silly notion.'

There were fifteen impressions of *The Collected Poems* (all of them containing misprints, though some corrections were made) printed by Jonathan Cape until 1955; and the type was reset in 1960, still with two errors in punctuation in the text. Following a protracted discussion over the years in *The Times Literary Supplement*, an error-free printing was finally published by Cape in 1971. A paperback appeared in 1967, and it too was not without misprints.

Penguin Books issued an edition in 1956, with an introduction by John Sparrow (reprinted in 1961).

The American edition, first published on 15 March 1940 by Henry Holt and Company (later Holt, Rinehart and Winston), has had a complicated history. Its early printings had numerous variations from the English edition and misprints; it too was involved in the textual and editing controversy in the *TLS* and other periodicals. One result was the publication of the *Complete Poems: Centennial Edition*, with an Introduction by Basil Davenport and a History of the Text by Tom Burns Haber (New York: Holt, Rinehart and Winston, 1959), which went through at least three printings. The English publishers forced its withdrawal as unauthorized, and since the 1960s the American edition, under the Holt, Rinehart and Winston imprint, in both clothbound and paperback, has followed the text and John Carter's note of the Jonathan Cape edition.

15
LETTERS TO E. H. BLAKENEY
(1941)

Letters from A. E. Housman to E. H. Blakeney. Of eighteen copies printed at Mr Blakeney's Private Press, Winchester, 1941, this is no. 8.

229 × 178 mm. Pale green wrappers, stitched; printed on the front cover: Housman Letters. 8 leaves.

Printed on one side of the paper only, this little pamphlet contains six letters dated 25 Nov. 1930, 22 April 1932, 27 April 1932, 28 April 1933, 17 Aug. 1934, 20 Dec. 1935, all written from Trinity College. Three brief notes are printed on the last leaf. The first two letters and the last are reprinted in *The Letters of A. E. Housman* (No. 24, below).

16
SELECTED POEMS
(1942?)

The Selected Poems of A. E. Housman. Editions for the Armed Services, Inc., a non-profit organization established by the Council on Books in Wartime, New York. [No date.]

95 × 140 mm. Paper wrappers, stapled, printed in yellow, red, white, blue, and black on the front and back covers; on front: M-1, Selected Poems, A. E. Housman, Armed Services Edition . . . U.S. Government Property, Not for sale. 128 pages.

Contains all of *The Collected Poems* except five poems: *A Shropshire Lad* XXV and LVI, *Last Poems* IX and XXXVIII, and *More Poems* XL. Contains John Carter's Note on the Text, and About the Author (two pages) by Louis Untermeyer (from *Modern British Poetry*).

Numbered M-1, this book was the first of the Armed Services Editions printed for free distribution overseas to American servicemen in World War II.

17

A.E.H. W.W.
(1944)

A.E.H. W.W. One of 12 copies, printed in 1944.

150 × 110 mm. Folded, without wrapper. 4 pages.

This tiny pamphlet, with an Explanatory Note signed E. H. B.[lakeney] on p. [2], contains on p. [3] a letter from Housman to The Midland Bank, dated 3 Nov. 1930, contributing 20 guineas to the Sir William Watson Testimonial Fund Account.

18

THE MANUSCRIPT POEMS
(1955)

The Manuscript Poems of A. E. Housman: Eight Hundred Lines of Hitherto Uncollected Verse from the Author's Notebooks. Edited by Tom Burns Haber. Minneapolis: The University of Minnesota Press, 1955.

215 × 137 mm. 80 leaves. Reddish brown cloth, lettered in gilt on spine. Issued in green dust-jacket, printed in white and green.

19

THIRTY LETTERS TO WITTER BYNNER
(1957)

Thirty Housman Letters to Witter Bynner. Edited by Tom Burns Haber. New York: Alfred A. Knopf, 1957.

230 × 140 mm. 24 leaves. Decorated boards, with blue cloth backstrip, lettered in gilt on spine.

700 copies, of which 600 were for the friends of Blanche and Alfred Knopf, Christmas 1957, and 100 for Witter Bynner and Tom Burns Haber.

Of these 30 letters, dated from 5 April 1903 to 12 October 1935, nine are reprinted in *The Letters of A. E. Housman* (see No. 24). The letters are now in Harvard University Library.

26

20
TO JOSEPH ISHILL:
FIVE UNPUBLISHED LETTERS
(1959)

A. E. Housman to Joseph Ishill: Five Unpublished Letters. By William White. 1859–1959. Published & Printed by The Oriole Press. Berkeley Heights, New Jersey, 1959.

200 × 117 mm. 10 leaves. Decorated paper-covered wrappers, in brown on cream-colored paper, with a tan slip (giving title and author) pasted at top of front cover.

54 copies for private distribution. The letters are also in *A Centennial Memento / With Excerpts from A Shropshire Lad and Fragment of a Greek Tragedy. . . . Including Five Letters to Joseph Ishill, With Commentary by William White* (Berkeley Heights: The Oriole Press, 1959, 50 copies), and previously appeared in the *American Book Collector*, Vol. IX, No. 5, pp. 9–10, January 1959.

Of these five letters, dated from 17 September 1930 to 26 December 1933, three are reprinted in *The Letters of A. E. Housman* (see No. 24). The letters are now in Harvard University Library.

21
SELECTED PROSE
(1961)

A. E. Housman, Selected Prose. Edited by John Carter. Cambridge: At the University Press, 1961.

185 × 122 mm. 112 leaves. Black cloth, lettered in gilt on spine. Issued in a white dust-jacket, printed in black and purple.

The text is preceded by a preface by John Carter and is followed by notes, mainly bibliographical, and an index.

The text contains *Introductory Lecture*; material from three prefaces (Manilius I, Manilius V, Juvenal); 18 reviews, classical papers and letters to the press; *The Application of Thought to Textual Criticism*, two biographical pieces (J. M. Image, Arthur Platt), four ceremonial addresses (Trinity College, Sir James George Frazer, Condolence to King George V, Congratulations to King George V); *The Name and Nature of Poetry*; and (in an appendix, from an unpublished typescript) three paragraphs of a paper on Matthew Arnold.

Selected Prose was published 20 October 1961 in both cloth-bound and paperback editions. An American edition, published by the Cambridge University Press, New York, has the line, 'Reprinted in the United States of America,' on the verso of the title-page. The book was reprinted, with corrections, in 1962.

22

THE MAKING OF A SHROPSHIRE LAD: A MANUSCRIPT VARIORUM
(1966)

The Making of A Shropshire Lad: A Manuscript Variorum. By Tom Burns Haber, Editor of the Centennial Edition of A. E. Housman's Poetry. Seattle and London: University of Washington Press, 1966.

235 × 150 mm. 169 leaves. Black cloth, lettered in gilt on red cloth on the spine. Issued in a pale buff dust-jacket, printed in black and red.

Contains an introduction on the composition of *A Shropshire Lad*, a selected bibliography (of 11 items), the texts of the 63 lyrics, with MS drafts from Housman's notebooks (on pages facing the lyrics). There are three errors in the texts of Housman's lyrics: XXXVII, 20, 'then' for 'than'; XLIII, 1, missing comma at end; and LXII, 31, 'half-way' for 'half way'.

23
THE CONFINES OF CRITICISM
(1969)

A. E. Housman, The Confines of Criticism: The Cambridge Inaugural 1911. The Complete Text with Notes by John Carter. Cambridge: At the University Press, 1969.

184 × 123 mm. 28 leaves. Black cloth with rough speckled yellow, lettered in gilt on the spine. Issued in a pale yellow-green dust-jacket printed in dark green.

Contains a preface by John Carter, a note on the text, and (following the text) an appendix, 'Shelley, Swinburne and Housman,' digested from a *Times Literary Supplement* article by John Carter and John Sparrow, 21 November 1968, pp. 1318–1319. This contains part of a letter from Housman, dated 21 September 1929, reprinted in full in *The Letters of A. E. Housman* (see No. 24).

The Confines of Criticism was published 11 November 1969. It contains misprints on pp. 7, 8, 21, 22, 23, 24, 42. 'Housman's Cambridge Inaugural,' minus a short paragraph, was first published in *The Times Literary Supplement*, 9 May 1968, pp. 475–477, followed by a note by John Carter; 25 copies were printed for private circulation by Mr. Carter. ('Meyor' for 'Mayor' is misprinted on p. 477.)

24
THE LETTERS
(1971)

The Letters of A. E. Housman. Edited by Henry Maas. London: Rupert Hart-Davis, 1971.

226 × 146 mm. 240 leaves. Maroon cloth, lettered in gilt on the spine. Issued in a red dust-jacket, printed in white and black.

Preceding the text of 882 chronologically arranged letters dated from 1875 to 1936 are Henry Maas's preface, manuscript and other locations, biographical table, and family chart, followed by (at the end) a select bibliography of 29 items, an index of recipients, and general index.

'I have been able to trace altogether some 1500,' Mr. Maas writes in his preface, 'and of these I print about half. With certain exceptions I have excluded only short notes dealing with appointments and minor matters of business, and letters whose contents is repeated in others. A small number of letters has not been available to me—notably those to Housman's greatest friend, Moses Jackson.'

Published in America by Harvard University Press, Cambridge, Massachusetts, in 1971 (printed in Great Britain), with differences only on the title-page, verso, spine, and dust-wrapper.

25

POETRY AND PROSE: A SELECTION
(1971)

A. E. Housman. Poetry and Prose: A Selection. Edited by F. C. Horwood. London: Hutchinson Educational, 1971.

185 × 120 mm. 128 leaves. Green and white paperback, printed in black on spine and front and back covers. Published October 1971, reprinted October 1972.

Contains an introduction, a biographical outline, 100 poems (from *A Shropshire Lad*, *Last Poems*, and *More Poems*), a translation (from *Oedipus Coloneus*), notes (some from Housman's notebooks) on the poems and the translation, two appendices, containing 'Fragment of a Greek Tragedy', Hugh Kingsmill's parody, and extracts from *Introductory Lecture*, Books I and V of Manilius, and *The Name and Nature of Poetry*, a selected bibliography (11 items), and indexes of first lines and titled poems.

There are about 20 misprints and errors, the most serious the date of Housman's death (26 October 1936 instead of 30 April [p. 43]).

26

THE CLASSICAL PAPERS
(1972)

The Classical Papers of A. E. Housman. Collected and Edited by J. Diggle & F. R. D. Goodyear. Volume I 1882–1897 . . . Volume II 1897–1914 . . . Volume III 1915–1936. Cambridge: At the University Press, 1972.

227 × 148 mm. 3 volumes, 675 leaves, plus frontispiece reproduction of the Francis Dodd portrait of A.E.H. at 67. Gray cloth, maroon tops, lettered in gilt on red cloth on spine. Issued in dustjackets of light buff paper, printed in maroon (Vol. I), blue (Vol. II), and brown (Vol. III).

Contains, following a brief preface, a list of editions consulted, and abbreviations, 174 classical articles and reviews from a variety of academic journals, plus 20 pieces in an appendix (reports of papers read to the Cambridge Philological Society, contributions to papers and books of other scholars, and items unsuited to inclusion in the body of the work). At the end are a list of A.E.H.'s classical papers, and indexes of passages, words, and topics.

27

FIFTEEN LETTERS TO WALTER ASHBURNER
(1976)

A. E. Housman. Fifteen Letters to Walter Ashburner. Edinburgh: The Tragara Press, MDCCCCLXXVI.

225 × 142 mm. 18 leaves. Blue wrappers, stitched, printed in black. 125 copies (100 for sale).

Following an untitled introduction (by Alan Bell) and accompanied by notes to 12 of the letters, are 15 letters, dating from 17 Nov. 1898 to 27 Dec. 1930.

31

28
HOUSMAN ON PLAUTUS
(1979)

Housman on Plautus: Manuscript Notes in the *Rudens* of Friedrich Marx (1928). Leiden: E. J. Brill [1979].

250 × 162 mm. 16 leaves. Pale blue wrappers, stapled, printed in blue. 600 copies, of which 500 were for the participants of the Congress of the International Federation of Societies of Classical Studies, Budapest, September 1979.

Following an untitled introduction (by R. Smitskamp) are about 125 Housman marginalia beside the relevant passages in Marx's edition of the *Rudens* of Plautus.

CONTRIBUTIONS TO BOOKS

29

Three Translations from the Greek

(1890)

Odes from the Greek Dramatists. Translated into lyric
metres by English poets and scholars. Edited by Alfred
W. Pollard. London: David Stott, 1890.

Housman's contributions are on p. 15 (*Septem contra Thebas*, 16
lines); pp. 85, 87 (*Oedipus Coloneus*, 42 lines); and pp. 109, 111
(*Alcestis*, 44 lines): all signed in full. The versions were specially
written for the book, not gathered from elsewhere.

There are variant bindings of this parchment-bound duodecimo,
of which that with the gold medallion on the front cover is almost
certainly the earlier (see *Bibliographical Notes and Queries*, Vol. II,
No. 4, p. 10, May 1936, and Vol. II, No. 6, p. 4, July 1936, for
further detail and argument).

There was also an issue on large (very large) paper, limited to 50
copies, signed by the editor.

Part of the edition was sent for distribution in the United States,
and these copies, otherwise identical with the medallioned London
issue, have the imprint on title-page and spine of A.C. McClurg &
Co., of Chicago.

Numerous reprintings of these translations, mostly American, are
listed by White, with a correction (by A.E.H.) (p. 32). *Collected
Poems*, pp. 243–247.

33

30
Testimonials
(1892)

Testimonials in Favour of Alfred Edward Housman . . .
a Candidate for the Professorship of Latin in University
College, London. Cambridge: Printed at the University
Press, 1892.

215 × 135 mm. Stitched, without wrappers. 12 leaves.

Pp. 3, 4 carry Housman's letter to the Council, dated 19 April 1892,
presenting himself as a candidate, and setting out his record as a
scholar up to that date. This is followed by an *Index* and seventeen
testimonials from the following scholars: Henry Nettleship, J. E. B.
Mayor, R. Y. Tyrrell, Arthur Palmer, Lewis Campbell, T. Herbert
Warren, Robinson Ellis, T. C. Snow, Herbert Millington, Alfred
W. Pollard, Henry Jackson, Joseph B. Mayor, A. W. Verrall, J. S.
Reid, G. M. Edwards, B. L. Gildersleeve, and N. Wecklein.

We can locate only three copies of this pamphlet (University
College, London, A. S. F. Gow, John Carter). It is understood that
two or three others were found among Housman's papers, but
their disposal was not recorded. There is no copy in the University
Library, Cambridge, nor in the library of Trinity College. At St.
John's College, Oxford, is a contemporary typescript (and its
carbon copy), with Wecklein's letter in MS transcript. The original
testimonial letters were destroyed by enemy action during the last
war.

31
Ibis in Postgate
(1894)

Corpus Poetarum Latinorum a se aliisque denuo recog-
nitorum et brevi lectionum varietate instructorum editit
Iohannes Percival Postgate. Tom. i . . . Londini:
Sumptibus G. Bell et filiorum, MDCCCXCIII.

Pp. 590–595 contain, among the poetry of Ovid, 'Ibis, recognitus
ab Aluredo E. Housman'. This is reprinted on pp. 287–301 of P.

Ovidi Nasonis Opera ex Corpore Poetarum Latinorum a Johanne Percival Postgate. Editio separatim typis impressa. Tomus III. London, G. Bell et filii; Cantabrigiae, Deighton, Bell et soc., MDCCCXCVIII.

Listed in Gow (p. 71), and in D. S. Robertson's life of A. E. Housman in *The Dictionary of National Biography . . . 1931–1940* (Oxford University Press, 1949), pp. 449–453; referred to in a note to Juvenal (No. 4) in Carter-Sparrow, 1952.

32
Diffugere Nives
(1897)

The Quarto. A Volume Artistic, Literary and Musical, Volume III. London: J. S. Virtue & Co., 1897.

This quarto was issued in two styles of binding: green cloth, title and design in gilt, and pale blue-green paper boards, title and design in black.

On p. 95 is the first printing of *Diffugere Nives* ('The snows are fled away, leaves on the shaws'). It is signed in full.

This is Housman's only published translation from the Latin— Horace, *Odes*, IV, 7. A letter to *The Times* (5 May 1936) from a lady who had attended his lectures at Cambridge perhaps explains this singularity. 'One morning in May 1914, when the trees in Cambridge were covered with blossom, he reached in his lecture Ode 7 in Horace's Fourth book, "Diffugere nives, redeunt iam gramina campis". This ode he dissected with the usual display of brilliance, wit, and sarcasm. Then for the first time in two years he looked up at us, and in quite a different voice said: "I should like to spend the last few minutes considering this ode simply as poetry." Our previous experience of Professor Housman would have made us sure that he would regard such a proceeding as beneath contempt. He read the ode aloud with deep emotion, first in Latin and then in an English translation of his own. "That", he said hurriedly, almost like a man betraying a secret, "I regard as the most beautiful poem in ancient literature", and walked quickly out of the room.'

Reprinted in *The Trinity Magazine* (Cambridge), Vol. III, No. 2, p. 37 (March 1922); *More Poems* V, with small differences of text; *Collected Poems*, p. 163, the original text restored.

33

The Oracles

(1903)

The Venture. An Annual of Art and Literature. Edited by Laurence Housman and W. Somerset Maugham. London: At John Baillie's, 1903.

4to grey pictorial boards, holland back.

On p. 39 is the first printing of *The Oracles* (''Tis mute, the word they went to hear'), signed in full.

The title is actually given at the head of the text as *The Oracle*, but this was a misprint, which Housman corrected in his own copy. He also deleted a superfluous comma in line 2.

Reprinted, *Last Poems* XXV.

34

The Sydney Address

(1903)

Record of the Jubilee Celebrations of the University of Sydney. September 30th, 1902. Sydney: William Brooks & Co., Ltd., 1903.

8vo cream boards lettered in gilt.

On p. 144 is a Latin address from University College, London, signed by its president. This was composed by Housman (see Gow, p. 80, note 1).

Mr. Gow wrote (loc. cit.): 'I suppose that as Professor of Latin at University College he may have been called upon for other such

36

addresses.' A Latin Address to Dublin University, July 1892, printed in broadsheet form, and found among his papers, was formerly considered possibly to be by him, but was in fact composed by J. P. Postgate. (It was reprinted in Postgate's *Translation and Translations: Theory and Practice* [London, 1922].)

35
Astronomy
(1904)

Wayfarer's Love. Contributions from Living Poets edited by the Duchess of Sutherland. Westminster: Archibald Constable, 1904.

Small 4to, green cloth decorated in gilt. Also 100 copies on large paper, bound in vellum, numbered and signed by the editor.

On p. 65 appears the first printing of *Astronomy* ('The Wain upon the northern steep'), signed in full.

Reprinted *Last Poems* XVII.

36
Juvenal in Postgate
(1905)

Corpus Poetarum Latinorum a se aliisque denuo recognitorum et brevi lectionum varietate instructorum editit Iohannes Percival Postgate. Tom. ii . . . Londini: Sumptibus G. Bell et filiorum, MDCCCV.

Pp. 532–564 contain: 'D. Iuni Iuuenalis saturae recognitae ab Aluredo E. Housman'.

Listed in Gow (p. 71), and in D. S. Robertson in *D.N.B.* . . . . *1931–1940*, pp. 449–453; referred to in a note to Juvenal (No. 4) in Carter–Sparrow, 1952, p. 29.

37

37
Address to H. M. Butler
(1913)

387 × 288 mm. 2 leaves. Privately printed in red and black, without imprint (but at the Cambridge University Press).

Anonymous. The first page carries the arms of Trinity College, the recipient's name, &c.; the second carries the text of the address; the third, a list of the signatories (the Fellows of the College, headed by the Vice-Master). The fourth page is blank.

Reprinted (and first published) in J. R. M. Butler's *Henry Montagu Butler, Master of Trinity College, Cambridge 1886–1918: A Memoir*, by His Son (London: Longmans, Green and Co., 1925), pp. 193–194.

38
Address to Henry Jackson
(1919)

301 × 204 mm. 2 leaves. Privately printed, without imprint (but at the Cambridge University Press).

Anonymous. The first page opens with 'Trinity College/14 July 1919/Dear Jackson/The present year, in which your eightieth birthday' &c. The second page carries the conclusion of the letter and two columns of signatories (Fellows and officers of the College). The third and fourth pages are blank.

Reprinted (and first published) in R. St John Parry's *Henry Jackson, O.M., Vice-Master of Trinity College & Regius Professor of Greek in the University of Cambridge: A Memoir* (Cambridge: At the University Press, 1926), pp. 115–116.

39
'Oh stay at home, my lad, and plough'
(1919)
A Tribute to Thomas Hardy O. M. June 2 1919.

Manuscript volume in the Thomas Hardy Memorial Collection in the Dorset County Museum. No title-page, but the inscription on the cover reads: A TRIBUTE TO | THOMAS HARDY O. M. | TH [inter-woven initials] | JUNE 2 1919 | .

The pages are not numbered, but disregarding several blank pages before an address to Hardy, on page [79] is a 10-line poem, beginning, 'Oh stay at home, my lad, and plough', signed A. E. Housman.

Reprinted in exactly the same form as *Last Poems* XXXVIII.

40
Address to Sir James George Frazer
(1921)

Address to Sir James George Frazer, LL.D., D.C.L., Litt.D., on the occasion of the foundation, in his honour, of the Frazer Lectureship in Social Anthropology in the Universities of Oxford, Cambridge, Glasgow, and Liverpool. Anno Domini MCMXXI.

258 × 170 mm. 10 leaves. Privately printed. Mottled brown wrappers, printed in black. The first two and last two leaves blank. At foot of p. [16] is the imprint 'Printed at S. Dominic's Press, Ditchling'. Anonymous.

Published in *The Frazer Lectures, 1922–32, by divers hands* (London: The Macmillan Company, 1932), pp. xi–xii.

41
Biographical Preface to Platt's *Essays*
(1927)

Nine Essays by Arthur Platt. With a preface by A. E. Housman. Cambridge: At the University Press, 1927.

8vo red cloth. Of the first (and only) edition 750 copies were printed.

Issued in a grey dust-jacket, printed in red and black.

Housman's preface occupies pp. [v]–xi.

In a letter to *The Times* of 9 November 1936, Dr. Francis Pember wrote: 'A colleague and great friend of Housman's at University College, London, was the late Arthur Platt, Professor of Greek there [from 1894 until his death].' Housman and Platt infused 'a certain liveliness' into the serious pages of the *Journal of Philology*. . . . In reference to [which] Housman made these two lines, which deserve not to be forgotten:

> 'Philology was tame, and dull, and flat:
> God said "Let there be larks", and there was Platt.'[1]

The extensive series of letters from Housman to Platt were burnt after the latter's death, but one survived: see *The Letters of A. E. Housman* (No. 24), p. 144.

The preface is reprinted in *Selected Prose* (No. 21), pp. 154–160, as 'Arthur Platt'.

[1] These lines were first printed in R. W. Chambers's *Man's Unconquerable Mind: Studies of English Writers, from Bede to A. E. Housman and W. P. Ker* (London and Toronto: Jonathan Cape, 1939), p. 362, with three variations in pointing.

BIOGRAPHIES, ETC., SOME CONTAINING ORIGINAL MATERIAL

42
Laurence Housman's *Seven Young Goslings*
(1898)

The Story of the Seven Young Goslings. By Laurence Housman. Illustrated by Mabel Dreamer. London, Glasgow & Dublin: Blackie & Son Limited [1898].

P. 7 contains a quatrain:

> Entombed in a wolf was
>   Her husband the gander,
> And the painful event had
>   Completely unmanned her.

Laurence Housman (*A.E.H.*, pp., 75–76) says: 'I generally sent to [Alfred] for criticism all my books of verse before publication; and because he took the trouble to read and to suggest improvements, one of these books, *The Mother Goose and her Seven Young Goslings*, has in it a couplet of his own composing, in place of what he was kind enough to say were the only two bad lines in the whole poem. The couplet which he sent me and which I gratefully accepted was this:

> Entombed in a wolf was her husband the gander,
> And the painful event had completely unmanned her.

—a small but kindly bit of collaboration which greatly pleased me.'

Laurence Housman's *Back Words and Fore Words* (London: Jonathan Cape, 1945, p. 24) contains a third variant of A.E.H.'s and L.H.'s collaboration:

> Entombed in a wolf
> Was her husband the gander,
>   And the painful event
> Had completely unmanned her.

Back Words and Fore Words gives 1898 as the date of the *Goslings*; the British Library gives 1899.

43
Gerard Manley Hopkins's *Poems*
(1918)

Poems of Gerard Manley Hopkins now first published. Edited with notes by Robert Bridges, Poet Laureate. London: Humphrey Milford (At the Oxford University Press), (1918).

P. [v] contains a dedication to Bridges's mother, which the Poet Laureate asked Housman to translate into Latin; it is reprinted in later editions, Second, 1930, p. xix; Third (First American), 1948, p. 3. (See Simon Nowell-Smith, 'Housman Inscriptions', *The Times Literary Supplement*, 6 November 1959, p. 643.)

44
A. Edward Newton's *This Book-Collecting Game*
(1928)

This Book-Collecting Game. By A. Edward Newton . . Boston: Little, Brown and Company, 1928.

P. 254 contains an undated letter (written after 1898) to Paul Lemperly. Reprinted in *The Letters of A. E. Housman* (see No. 24), dated 11 December 1899.

45
Sir William Rothenstein's *Men and Memories*
(1932)

Men and Memories: Recollections of William Rothenstein, 1900–22 [Vol. 2] . . . London: Faber & Faber Limited (1932).

P. 187 contains a 7-line nonsense verse, beginning 'O why do you walk through the fields in boots', a parody of Frances Cornford; the volume was reprinted by Faber & Faber, 1934; and in America by Coward-McCann, New York, 1932.

The parody in William Rothenstein's letter, dated 22 March 1910, is reprinted in *The Letters of A. E. Housman* (see No. 24).

46

Grant Richards's *Author Hunting*
(1934)

Author Hunting By an Old Literary Sportsman: Memories of Years Spent Mainly in Publishing 1897–1925. By Grant Richards. London: Hamish Hamilton, 1934.

Pp. 99, 268, 268–269 contain three letters, dated 17 Aug. 1906, 5 Jan. 1921, 22 April 1922, to Grant Richards. They are reprinted in Grant Richards's *Housman: 1897–1936* (No. 55, below), pp. 73, 184 (completed by an additional sentence); and in *The Letters of A. E. Housman* (see No. 24).

An American edition of *Author Hunting* was published, with a rearranged title-page, by Coward-McCann, Inc., New York, in 1934; and a new English edition by The Unicorn Press, London, in 1960, with a shortened title.

47

Mrs. E. W. Symons's *Memories* and *More Memories*
(1936)

Memories of A. E. Housman. By Mrs. E. W. Symons. From the Magazine of King Edward's School, Bath, *The Edwardian*, Vol. 17, No. 3, Sept., 1936 . . . Bath: J. Grant Mellush [1936].

47a

More Memories of A. E. H. By Mrs. E. W. Symons. Reprinted by *The Edwardian* Magazine, Bath, December 1936.

Pp. 2, 3, 4, 5 of *Memories* contain 7 light verses, beginning 'Little Miss Muffet sat on a tuffet' (4 lines), 'There is Hallelujah Hannah' (8 lines), 'As I was walking slowly' (24 lines), 'Amelia mixed some mustard' (8 lines), 'The Grizzly Bear is huge and wild' ('Infant Innocence', 4 lines), 'To meet a bad lad on the African waste' ('The African Lion,' 12 lines), and ' "In the back back garden Thomasina" ' ('The Amphisbaena,' 21 lines).

P. 1 of *More Memories* contains 2 light verses, beginning 'A tail behind, a trunk in front' ('The Force of Habit,' 8 lines) and 'O emperor Heliogabalus' ('Heliogabalus,' 6 lines). 'The Force of Habit' has a correction in ink of line 3 from 'A tail in front' to 'A tail before'.

'Hallelujah Hannah', and 'Amelia mixed some mustard' (with variant readings) are reprinted in Laurence Housman's *A.E.H.* (see No. 52), pp. 133 and 235, as are 'Infant Innocence' (with variant readings), p. 236, 'In the back back garden Thomasina', p. 233, and 'A tail behind, a trunk in front' (with variant readings), p. 236; and 'O emperor Heliogabalus' is reprinted in John Pugh's *Bromsgrove and the Housmans* (see No. 65), p. xxvi.

48

Laurence Housman's *The Unexpected Years*
(1936)

The Unexpected Years. By Laurence Housman. Illustrated. Indianapolis and New York: The Bobbs-Merrill Company, 1936.

Pp. 86, 89 contain two verses, beginning 'At the door of my own little hovel' and 'Breathe, my lute, beneath my fingers'. P. 137 contains the fragment of a letter, undated, to Laurence Housman.

'At the door of my own little hovel' is reprinted in Laurence Housman's *A.E.H.* (No. 52), p. 58, and the first four lines of

44

'Breathe, my lute, beneath my fingers' in the *Bromsgrove Memorial Supplement* (see No. 50) and in its entirety in Laurence Housman's *A.E.H.*, p. 38. The fragmentary letter is reprinted in Laurence Housman's *A.E.H.*, pp. 76–77, and *The Letters of A. E. Housman* (No. 24), pp. 40–41.

An English edition of *The Unexpected Years* was published by Jonathan Cape, London, in 1937.

49
A. S. F. Gow's *A Sketch*
(1936)

A. E. Housman: A Sketch, Together with a List of His Writings and Indexes to His Classical Papers. By A. S. F. Gow, Fellow of Trinity College, Cambridge. Cambridge: At the University Press, 1936.

Opposite p. 32 is the facsimile of a letter, dated 20 Jan. 1928, to A. S. F. Gow; on p. 31 is a couplet (not published elsewhere); and there are quotations from Housman's conversations and passages from letters. The letter to Gow is reprinted in *The Letters of A. E. Housman* (No. 24).

An American edition of *A Sketch* was published by The Macmillan Company, New York, in 1936.

50
Bromsgrove Memorial Supplement
(1936)

Alfred Edward Housman: Recollections. By Katharine E. Symons, A. W. Pollard, Laurence Housman, R. W. Chambers, Alan Ker, A. S. F. Gow, John Sparrow. A. E. H., Bromsgrove School, 1870–1877. Bromsgrove School for the Housman Memorial fund, 1936.

Pp. 15, 17, 18, 22, 22, 23, and 43 contain various light and other verses: '"Look here! look here!" one of them cries' ('Feathered conversation,' 14 lines), 'The thin blue clouds that pall the dying day' (2 lines), 'Summer! and over brooding lands' ('Summer,' 21 lines), 'Of old the little Busy Bee' (8 lines), 'The oyster is found in the ocean' (12 lines), 'Oft when the night is chilly' (16 lines), 'Birds in their little nests agree' (4 lines, two versions).

The 'Feathered conversation' is reprinted in full, 104 lines, in a letter to Lucy Housman, postmarked 22 April 1875, in *The Letters of A. E. Housman* (No. 24).

'Summer' is reprinted in Laurence Housman's *A.E.H.* (No. 52), pp. 33–34, and in Norman Marlow's *A. E. Housman: Scholar and Poet* (No. 62, below), p. 14.

This Supplement to the October 1936 *Bromsgrovian* appeared in three English printings: a limited and numbered edition of 250 copies (October 1936), not for sale; a limited edition of 500 copies (November 1936), and a third edition (November 1936).

An American edition, 235 × 155 mm, dark blue cloth, lettered in gilt on spine and front cover, 48 leaves, plus frontispiece and illustrations, issued in a dust wrapper printed in dark blue, was published by Henry Holt and Company, New York, in 1937.

51

Cyril Clemens's *An Evening with A. E. Housman* (1937)

An Evening with A. E. Housman. By Cyril Clemens. With a Foreword by Padraic Colum. Webster Groves, Missouri: International Mark Twain Society, 1937.

Pp. [1]–2, [5]–[6], 7, 19 contain letters to Cyril Clemens, dated 2 March 1936, 2 February 1927, 1 August 1930, 26 March 1933. All except the letter of 1 August 1930 are reprinted in *The Letters of A. E. Housman* (No. 24).

The last three letters originally appeared in *The Mark Twain Quarterly*, Vol. I, No. 2, pp. [8], 9, 22, Winter 1936. The letter of 2 March 1936 was reprinted in Cyril Clemens's *My Cousin Mark Twain* (Emmaus, Pa: Rodale Press, 1939), p. 212.

52

Laurence Housman's *A.E.H.*

(1937)

A. E. H. Some Poems, Some Letters and a Personal Memoir by his Brother Laurence Housman. London: Jonathan Cape, [26 November] 1937.

Pp. 19–133 contain a Memoir, which includes 15 hitherto un-printed letters and 11 early poems.

Pp. 127–207 contain a selection of 106 letters. The letters to Mr. Houston Martin, an American, from which selections are printed at pp. 193–198, had been printed in full in *The Yale Review*, Winter 1937, pp. 283–303. The rest of the letters had not hitherto been printed.

Pp. 214–226 contain 18 poems, called 'Additional Poems', of which two had been printed before: No. V (a four-line stanza inscribed in Walter Headlam's copy of Manilius I) in *The Times Literary Supplement* 31 October 1936 and No. XVIII ('Oh who is that young sinner with the handcuffs on his wrists?') in *John O'London's Weekly*. (See No. 98.)

Pp. 230–247 contain 13 Light Verse and Parodies, of which five had been already printed in Mrs. Symons's contributions to *The Edwardian* and *The Bromsgrove Memorial Supplement* (No. 50).

Verses by Housman not hitherto reprinted occur at the following pages: p. 32 ('The city is silent and solemn'); p. 252 ('Joy, take my hand, talk to my heart').

96 letters are reprinted in *The Letters of A. E. Housman* (No. 24).

The verse, 'Gross weighs the mounded marl,' p. 88, is reprinted in Norman Marlow, *A. E. Housman: Scholar and Poet* (No. 62), p. 179, Tom Burns Haber, *A. E. Housman* (No. 64), p. 45; and *Housman Society Journal*, Vol. 6, p. 13, 1980.

Published in America as *My Brother, A. E. Housman: Personal Recollections Together with Thirty Hitherto Unpublished Poems*, New York, Charles Scribner's Sons, 1938.

53
Percy Withers's *A Buried Life*
(1940)

A Buried Life: Personal Recollections of A. E. Housman. By Percy Withers. London: Jonathan Cape, 1940.

P. 66 contains a light verse, beginning 'It is a fearful thing to be / The Pope' (10 lines). There are also excerpts from 35 letters, all reprinted in full in *The Letters of A. E. Housman* (No. 24).

Some of this material originally appeared in *The New Statesman and Nation*, New Series, Vol. 11, pp. 700–702, 9 May 1936; reprinted in *The Living Age*, New York, Vol. 350, pp. 414–418, July 1936.

54
Clyde Kenneth Hyder's *Concordance*
(1940)

A Concordance to the Poems of A. E. Housman. Compiled and Edited by Clyde Kenneth Hyder. The University of Kansas. Lawrence, Kansas, 1940.

Includes all the poems in *The Collected Poems*, 'Light Verse and Parodies' in Laurence Housman's *A.E.H.*, the poems in Mrs. E. W. Symons's *Memories* and in the Bromsgrove Memorial Supplement, and a word list for *Fragment of a Greek Tragedy*.

55
Grant Richards's *Housman: 1897–1936*
(1941)

Housman: 1897–1936. By Grant Richards. With an Introduction by Mrs. E. W. Symons and Appendices by G. B. A. Fletcher and Others. Oxford University Press. London: Humphrey Milford, 1941.

Contains 462 letters, dated between 22 February 1898 and 18 March 1936, to Richards or his Press, plus five to Mrs. Richards in 1919, 1921, and 1922; letter (in two versions) to Sir James Barrie (pp.

384–385); one to M. Maurice Pollet, dated 5 February 1933 (pp. 267–274); and one to Mrs. E. W. Symons, 17 June 1879; a comic verse, 24 lines, beginning 'When bells are tolling' (p. 376); another comic verse, 20 lines, beginning 'As into the garden Elizabeth ran,' (opposite p. 54).

Folded, insided the back cover, is the facsimile of a family chart written out by A. E. Housman in 1908 for Col. Harold Chippindall, a relative who was preparing a much more extensive chart.

Of the letters to Grant Richards and his Press, 262 are reprinted in *The Letters of A. E. Housman* (No. 24), as are three to Mrs. Richards and the letter to M. Maurice Pollet.

An American edition, identified by 'Oxford University Press, New York, 1942', on the title-page, does not have the plate containing the comic verse, 'As into the garden Elizabeth ran'; and the family chart is printed on the last pages of the book, pp. [494]–[495].

56
G. H. Hardy's *Bertrand Russell & Trinity*
(1942)

Bertrand Russell & Trinity: A College Controversy of the Last War. By G. H. Hardy. Cambridge: Printed for the Author at the University Press, 1942.

Pp. 54–55 contain a letter, undated but written in 1919, to H. A. Hollond.

Reprinted in facsimile with a Foreword by C. D. Broad, Cambridge: At the University Press, 1970.

57
Sir E. Denison Ross's *Both Ends of the Candle*
(1943)

Both Ends of the Candle: The Autobiography of Sir E. Denison Ross. With a Foreword by Laurence Binyon. London: Faber and Faber Limited, Mcmxliii.

Contains a letter, dated 11 May 1901, to Sir Edwin Denison Ross. Reprinted in *Housman Society Journal*, Vol. 2, 1975, p. 33.

58
F. Brittain's *Arthur Quiller-Couch*
(1947)

Arthur Quiller-Couch: A Biographical Study of Q. By F. Brittain, M. A., Fellow of Jesus College, Cambridge. Cambridge: At the University Press, 1947.

P. 135 contains a letter, dated 9 May 1929, to Arthur Quiller-Couch.

Reprinted in *The Letters of A. E. Housman* (No. 64). The American edition of *Arthur Quiller-Couch*, published in 1948, is identified by the additional line, New York: The Macmillan Company.

59
Oliver Robinson's *Angry Dust*
(1950)

Angry Dust: The Poetry of A. E. Housman, A Critical Essay. By Oliver Robinson. Boston: Bruce Humphries, Inc., 1950.

P. 10 contains a facsimile of letter, dated 25 Nov. 1933, to Oliver Robinson.

60
George L. Watson's *A. E. Housman*
(1957)

A. E. Housman: A Divided Life. By George L. Watson. London: Rupert Hart-Davis, 1957.

P. 116 contains a mock-sentimental light verse, beginning 'From attics and sky-touching flats' (7 lines), sent to Mrs. Edith M. Wise for the Wise Family Visitor's Book, dated 12 April 1887.

50

An American edition was published by the Beacon Press, Boston, in 1958.

61

Maude M. Hawkins's *A. E. Housman:*
Man Behind a Mask
(1958)

A. E. Housman: Man Behind a Mask. By Maude M. Hawkins . . . Chicago: Henry Regnery Company, 1958.

Pp. 165, 187–189 contain a letter, dated 26 May 1908, to Laurence Housman, and seven letters (or excerpts), dated between 4 May 1916 and 12 Dec. 1933, to J. W. Mackail; but this book is so untrustworthy—with more than 200 misquotations—that one should consult *The Letters of A. E. Housman* (No. 24), in which all but one (for 23 March 1926) are reprinted. The letter to Laurence Housman exists only in Mrs. Hawkins's text, from which it was taken by Mr. Maas.

62

Norman Marlow's *A. E. Housman: Scholar and Poet*
(1958)

A. E. Housman: Scholar and Poet. By Norman Marlow. Minneapolis: The University of Minnesota Press, 1958.

Pp. 13–15, 171–179 contain reprintings of Housman juvenilia and nonsense verses, including 'The Oak,' 'Summer,' 'Breathe, my lute, beneath my fingers,' 'At the door of my own little hovel,' 'I knew a Cappadocian,' 'A tail behind, a trunk in front,' 'Fragment of a Poem on Latin Grammar,' 'Fragment of an English Opera,' and 'Gross weighs the mounded marl,' among others.

63

Exhibition Catalogue, *A. E. Housman: A Collection*
(1961)

A. E. Housman: A Collection of Manuscripts, Letters, Proofs, First Editions, Etc. Formed by H. B. Collamore

51

of West Hartford, Connecticut: Presented to the Lilly Library, Indiana University. Exhibition April 1–30, 1961.

Contains 4 lines in Latin with A.E.H.'s English translation from 'Iona', p. 5, letters: (16 February 1905), p. 6; (23 February 1929), p. 7; (21 February 1898), p. 8; (17 August 1906), p. 12; (12 September 1915), p. 13; (22 May 1931), p. 16; (7 July 1933 and 15 December 1930), p. 18. Also 18 unpublished verses, including informal rhymes (from the Wise family books), pp.22–32; and more letters: (30 July 1890), p. 26; (25 April 1905), p. 29; (30 April 1934), p. 32. All the letters except three (15 December 1930, 22 May 1931, and 1 July 1933) are reprinted in *The Letters of A. E. Housman* (No. 24, above).

64

Tom Burns Haber's *A. E. Housman*

(1967)

A. E. Housman. By Tom Burns Haber. Editor of the Centennial Edition of the Poetry of A. E. Housman. New York: Twayne Publishers, Inc., 1967.

Pp. 35–44 contain first book printings of five of the 13 Housman contributions to *Ye Rounde Table* (1878): 'The Sailor Boy' (also in *JEGP*, 1962—see No. 68), 'Tennyson in the Moated Grange' (also in *JEGP*), 'Punch and Jouida: A Novel,' 'Varsity Ballads—No. 1. Jones His Repartee,' 'Tempora Mutantur'; pp. 110–113 contain nine 'poems recovered from the notebooks,' now in the Library of Congress; and throughout the book are quotations from these notebooks.

65

John Pugh's *Bromsgrove and the Housmans*

(1974)

Bromsgrove and the Housmans. By John Pugh. Bromsgrove, Worcestershire: The Housman Society, 1974.

Pp. xviii–xxxii contain 'Iona' (218 lines, prefaced by four lines in Latin from Catullus), beginning 'Black spirits & white that mingle as they may'; eight miscellaneous verses, chiefly educational, 'What, little Arthur, do you know' (16 lines), 'O emperor Heliogabalus' (6 lines, reprinted from Mrs. E. W. Symons's *More Memories*, No. 47), 'The Latin author Lucan' (11 lines), 'The poet Diocletian' (9 lines), 'Morbid Matilda, or Over-Education' (8 lines, beginning 'Matilda drank a pebble'), 'Purple William, or The Liar's Doom' (20 lines, beginning 'The hideous hue which William is'), 'Aunts and Nieces, or Time and Space' (52 lines, beginning 'Some nieces won't, some nieces can't'); pp. lxxiv–lxxxvi contain 11 letters, dated from 4 April 1881 to 18 June 1934), to Kate (Katharine) Symons and Jeannie (Jane) Housman.

66

Richard Perceval Graves's *A. E. Housman*
(1979)

A. E. Housman: The Scholar-Poet. By Richard Perceval Graves. London and Henley: Routledge & Kegan Paul, 1979.

Pp. 33–34, 46–47, 71–72, 145, 195 contain parts of five light verses: 'And Minnie will look in the looking glass' (20 lines), 'By her bed-curtain' (14 lines), 'Oh decorate the station' and 'From attics and sky-touching flats' (4 and 7 lines), 'This is the house where Perkins dwelt' (9 lines), and 'Proposal for an edition of the Septuagint by M. R. James' (two verses, 4 lines each); p. 74, a diary entry (6 lines); pp. 143, 239, parts of two letters, 25 Dec. 1925, to Katharine Symons, and 28 Dec. 1924, to Pearce Higgins; and pp. 237–238, fragment of a verse, 'Once in the springing season' (8 lines). These are the longest or most important of the many pieces in the Graves volume of unpublished material by A. E. Housman.

An American edition was published by Charles Scribner's Sons, New York, in 1979.

CONTRIBUTIONS TO PERIODICALS

67
The Death of Socrates
(1874)

The Bromsgrove Messenger, 8 August 1874.

This issue of the local paper, p. 3, contains the first printing of *The Death of Socrates*, the poem with which Housman, then fifteen years of age and head of the Fourth Form, won the English verse prize at Bromsgrove School. It runs to 106 lines in rhymed couplets, beginning 'Though thou art free no more, though every trace'. The concluding 10 lines were reprinted by Mr. Laurence Housman in his *Memoir* (p. 31), and the entire poem, *PMLA* (New York), Vol. LXVIII, No. 4, pp. 913–914, September 1953.

A.E.H.'s composition for the previous year, *Sir Walter Raleigh*, which was unsuccessful, was published in *Etudes Anglaises* (Paris), Vol. VI, No. 4, pp. 346–349, November 1953. He won the prize again in 1875; but in this case the *Messenger* (Saturday, 31 July, p. 2) merely recorded the fact of the recitation, without giving the verses. The subject was *St. Paul on Mars Hill*. (See No. 90, below.)

68
Contributions to *Ye Rounde Table*
(1878)

Ye Rounde Table, Vol. 1, Nos. 1–6, 2 February–22 June 1878.

Subtitled *An Oxford and Cambridge Magazine*, this undergraduate periodical contains thirteen contributions by Housman, identified in the personal copy of Falconer Madan, who later became Bodley's Librarian. (The copy is now in the Sterling Library of Yale University.)

Housman's contributions are:
 1. 'The History of Crime: By A Gaul at Oxford,' No. 1, pp. 4–5.
 2. 'The History of Crime,' No. 2, pp. 19–20.
 3. 'The Sailor-Boy,' No. 2, p. 21.
 4. 'Tennyson in the Moated Grange,' No. 3, p. 35.
 5. 'Punch and Jouida: A Novel,' No. 3, pp. 41–43.
 6. 'Varsity Ballads.—No. 1. Jones His Repartee,' No. 4, pp. 51–52.
 7. 'Punch and Jouida,' No. 4, pp. 52–55.
 8. 'Varsity Ballads.—No. 2. Over to Rome,' No. 5, pp. 68–69.
 9. 'Under the Clock,' No. 5, pp. 72–74.
10. 'Hard Cases,' No. 5, pp. 75–77.
11. 'Tempora Mutantur,' No. 6, pp. 81–83.
12. 'The Eleventh Eclogue,' No. 6, pp. 87–90.
13. 'Under the Clock,' No. 6, pp. 90–93.

Two of the poems, 'The Sailor-Boy' and 'Tennyson in the Moated Grange' (plus two excerpts from the 'Varsity Ballads'), are reprinted in Tom Burns Haber's 'A. E. Housman and *Ye Rounde Table*,' *JEGP*, Vol. LXI, No. 4, pp. 797–809, 1962, with additional information about Housman and the periodical. For these and other reprintings, see Haber's *A. E. Housman* (No. 64).

69
Parta Quies
(1881)

Waifs and Strays: A Terminal Magazine of Oxford Poetry, Vol. II, No. VI, March 1881. Oxford: Blackwell; London: Simpkin Marshall, 1881.

On p. 23 is the first printing of *Parta Quies* ('Good-night; ensured release'), signed 'A. E. H.'

Reprinted, with several differences of text and under the title *Alta Quies*, in *More Poems* XLVIII. Restored to the original text and title in *Collected Poems*, p. 211.

70
New Year's Eve
(1881)

Waifs and Strays, Vol. III, No. VIII, November 1881.

On p. 54 is the first printing of *New Year's Eve* ('The end of the year fell chilly'), signed 'A. E. H.'

Reprinted in *Collected Poems*, p. 236.

These two artistically produced fascicles, in their cream wrappers printed in brown, contain all Housman's serious poetry to be printed during his Oxford period.[1] 'It is a wonder', says his brother (*Memoir*, p. 34), 'and something of a mystery that a writer so prolific of verse in his teens[2] should have produced so little during his twenties. Except for three poems written during his Oxford years (two of them published [Nos. 69 & 70]—the third, his attempt for the Newdigate Prize in 1879, 'Iona', not published [until 1974, see John Pugh's *Bromsgrove and the Housmans*, pp. xvii–xxiv, (No. 65)], I have not been able to discover, even in the four note-books into which he jotted down the beginnings and rough drafts of his poems, any trace of a poem of earlier date than 1890.'

71
A Morning with the Royal Family
(1882)

The Bromsgrovian. Bromsgrove: Printed for the Editor, at the 'Messenger' office, 1882. New Series, Vol. 1, No. 2, 15 February; and Vol. 1, No. 3, 29 March.

The first number contains (pp. 27–30) Chapters I to V, the second (pp. 52–59) Chapters V, concluded, to XI, of *A Morning with the Royal Family*.

---

[1] He also made thirteen humourous contributions to *Ye Rounde Table*, an undergraduate periodical. (See No. 68.)

[2] The reference is to verses circulated among the family, in manuscript, of which specimens are given in the *Memoir*.

CHAPTER II.

THE Royal family seated at breakfast when the king ran out after the pigs, consisted of the queen, princess Amelia (the eldest of the family), prince Henry (the heir apparent), and the baby. The moment her father left the room, princess Amelia drove her tea cup into the marmalade, extracted a large scoop, and swallowed it.

"Well I never!" said the queen, "Amelia!"

"Heaven helps those who help themselves, mamma," replied the princess, wiping her mouth with her pinafore.

The queen opened her mouth to rebuke this remark, but a bluebottle flying into it distracted her attention; and scarcely had she finished drowning the bluebottle in the slop basin when a terrific crash resounded through the palace.

"What an extraordinary noise," exclaimed the queen; "it sounded exactly like a cedar tree blowing down on a constitutional monarch. Henry, I wonder if anything has happened to your papa."

"If it has," said prince Henry, leaning back in his chair, "I hereby give a free pardon to all murderers and felons, and I lower the price of bread one penny per loaf, and I will have a damson pudding for lunch. I should like to commence my reign auspiciously, you know, mamma," said he, in a meditative way. He then took a slice of bread and jam in one hand, and his teacup in the other, and went out to see what had become of the king.

CHAPTER III.

AN incautious reader of the end of my first chapter might perhaps suppose that he found the king dead on the doorstep. But I did not say that the king was killed by the cedar tree; I merely said that he was succeeded by his son Henry X.; and so he was, when he died, which was fifteen years afterwards. He was not hurt by the cedar tree at all, he was only rather frightened and exceedingly angry, as it had killed the pigs, which he wanted to have the killing of to himself. He was therefore lying on the gravel and addressing the cedar tree in language which perhaps is best described by the poet Laureate in his beautiful poem on the occasion, beginning :—

> As I came over the windy lea
> The king was cursing the cedar tree,
> And the way his Majesty curse and swore,
> I never had heard such oaths before.

IV.   Page 28 of No. 71, showing the cancel-slip.
The words beneath are "Oh, God".

Of this anonymous skit, which contains some verse, mostly in the final chapter, Mr. Laurence Housman writes as follows (*Memoir*, p. 58): 'One Christmas (1879, I think), we attempted something more ambitious, which produced a memorable result. Each wrote a story, and on Christmas Eve, or thereabouts, the stories were read out to the assembled family. Alfred's contribution was a domestic sketch in verse and prose entitled "A Morning with the Royal Family", the opening sentence of which ran: "'Pigs on the front lawn again!' cried the King, 'Give me a cannon, somebody!' Nobody gave him a cannon, so seizing a teaspoon from the breakfast table he rushed from the apartment." This is the story—the only complete work of fiction, I think, which he ever produced[1]—which was published a year or two later, without his permission, in the Bromsgrove School Magazine, and has remained ever since a prized but rather private family possession, republication having been strictly forbidden by the author.[2] In the school it had a great success—even the Headmaster enjoyed it; but it contained two improprieties of a profane character—or what were thought to be so in those days; and, in order that none might be scandalized, the Headmaster caused little slips of paper to be pasted over the offending words, with harmless substitutes printed thereon. Of course, they were all picked away in no time, but the symbolic fig-leaves served their purpose, indicating a belated censorship for the satisfaction of school parents.'

Any collectors lucky enough to run down these flimsy octavos in pale blue wrappers should look for the slips on pp. 28 (see Plate II) and 29.

One of the sets of verses ('As I was a-walking among the grassy hay') was reprinted anonymously in *Ant Antics* (edited by Lady Cave; London: John Murray, 1933), p. 96, and again in Mrs. E. W. Symons's contribution to *The Edwardian* (see No. 47).

---

[1] A short sequel, written out for his brother Basil in 1931, survives in manuscript —'The only existing portion of my second work of fiction.'

[2] Reprinted since his death, however: *Town & Country* (New York), Vol. XCV, No. 4219, pp. 60–1, 114–15, December 1940; and in book-form, Green Horn Press, Los Angeles, 1941, 16 leaves, 125 copies. (See White, *The Library*, Fourth Series, Vol. XXIII, p. 32.)

72
Hendecasyllables
(1882)

The Bromsgrovian, Vol. I, No. 4, 25 May 1882.

On p. 92 is printed this set of Latin verses; 16 lines, beginning 'O quot fert Thetis, insularum ocelle': signed 'A. E. H.' They are a rendering of John Dryden's poem *Britain* ('Fairest isle, all isles excelling'), which follows them on the same page.

Reprinted in *The Classical Journal*, Vol. 50, No. 4, p. 160, January 1955; and in *A. E. Housman: Catalogue of an Exhibition on the Centenary of His Birth*, assembled by John Carter and Joseph W. Scott (London: University College London, 1959), p. 23. 'This', writes Mr. Gow (p. 77, note 3), 'and the elegiac dedication of the Manilius are the only Greek or Latin verses of Housman's I have seen . . . in the Cambridge Inaugural Lecture he defended verse-writing as being, unlike most forms of learning, an act of creation, and thereby enlivening and developing the faculties; but he had little taste for it himself.'

73
Fragment of a Greek Tragedy
(1883)

The Bromsgrovian, Vol. II, No. 5, 8 June 1883.

On pp. 107–109 is the first printing of *Fragment of a Greek Tragedy*, signed 'A. E. H.'

Gow (p. 76) gives references for the following reprints: *University College Gazette*, 1897; *Cornhill Magazine*, April 1901: *Trinity Magazine*, 1921; privately printed at the Snail's Pace Press, Amherst, U.S.A., 1925; *Yale Review*, 1928; *Apes and Parrots*, ed. J. C. Squire, 1928; *New York Herald-Tribune*, 1936. (Also in *High School Chronicle* [Girls' High School, Sydney, Australia], March 1917, pp. 17–18.)

'The text of this parody', Gow continues, 'was considerably altered before its second, and again before its third appearance. The

Cornhill text appears in *Apes and Parrots* and in the *New York Herald-Tribune*. The *Trinity Magazine* makes acknowledgements to the *Cornhill* but contains improvements in ll. 8 and 59 and differs in punctuation. The *Yale Review* speaks of recent changes by the author, but its text, apart from misprints in ll. 10 and 58, differs from that of the *Trinity Magazine* only in reverting to the punctuation of the *Cornhill*.'

Reprints not listed by Gow but cited by White (p. 32) include *The Living Age* (Boston), Vol. CCXXIX, No. 2967, pp. 437–439, 18 May 1901 (the *Cornhill* text, signed *A. E. Housman*); and two printings in pamphlet form, one by the Peter Pauper Press (Mt. Vernon, New York [1937], as a supplement to its edition of *A Shropshire Lad*) and one by the Branford College Press (New Haven, Conn., 1938).

Two more recent reprints are in *A Centennial Memento / With Excerpts from A Shropshire Lad and Fragment of a Greek Tragedy*. . . . (Berkeley Heights, New Jersey: The Oriole Press, 1959); and A. E. Housman, *Poetry and Prose: A Selection* (see No. 25), pp. 221–225.[1]

74

Hypermnestra

(1884)

The Bromsgrove Messenger, 24 May 1884.

This 'very freely rendered' verse translation from Horace, Ode 11, Book 3, was published on p. 3 of the local paper over the signature of E. H. B., apparently for 'Edward Housman, Bromsgrove', the poet's father, who 'improved' the poem and submitted it for publication. It was reprinted in *Modern Language Notes* (Johns Hopkins University), Vol. LXX, No. 2, pp. 103–104, February 1955; and (with slight variations) in *Housman Society Journal*, Vol. 5, pp. 30–31, 1979.

---

[1] Because this bibliography is not meant to be definitive—one must still consult Gow for his papers on Latin and Greek—I have omitted the amusingly vitriolic letter to *The Standard* (London), 14 March 1894, about Highgate Wood; furthermore, it is now printed in *The Letters of A. E. Housman* (No. 24), pp. 30–31.

75
R.L.S.
(1894)

The Academy, No. 1181, 22 December 1894.

These lines on the death of Robert Louis Stevenson were first printed on p. 533, signed in full.

This is the piece of which Gow wrote (p. 22): 'The Fitzwilliam Museum used to exhibit the manuscript of a poem by him, published in a periodical but not reprinted in either volume of verse; and when he gave the Museum the manuscript of *Last Poems* he retrieved and burnt the poem he wished forgotten.'

Reprinted on p. 41 of *In Praise of Stevenson, An Anthology*, Chicago: The Bookfellows, 1919; and *Collected Poems*, p. 239.

Also reprinted in a 4-page, 212 × 143 mm. pamphlet, undated, without imprint, in an edition of 50 copies 'for the friends of Vincent Starrett and Edwin B. Hill' after 1922.

76
Extract from a Didactic Poem on Latin Grammar
(1899)

University College (London) Gazette, 22 March 1899, Vol. II, No. 21.

On p. 34 is the first printing of these verses, beginning 'See on the cliff fair Adjectiva stand'. They originally formed the conclusion to a paper on Erasmus Darwin, whose style they imitate.

Reprinted in Laurence Housman's *A.E.H.*, pp. 245–247, with title 'Fragment of a Didactic Poem on Latin Grammar.' (see No. 52).

Illic jacet.

1

Oh hard is the bed they have made him,
　And common the blanket and cheap;
But there he will lie as they laid him:
　Where else could you trust him to sleep?

2

To sleep when the bugle is crying
　And cravens have heard and are brave,
When mothers and sweethearts are sighing
　And lads are in love with the grave

3

Oh dark is the chamber and lonely,
　And lights and companions depart;
But lief will he lose them, and only
　Behold the desire of his heart.

Part of an autograph manuscript of No. 77, written in 1915.

77
Illic Jacet
(1900)

The Academy, Vol. LXIII, 24 February 1900.

On p. 169 is printed for the first time *Illic Jacet* ('Oh hard is the bed they have made him'), signed in full.

77a

The Edwardian, Vol. VII, No. 19, December 1915 (see also No. 30).

On p. 453 the poem is reprinted under the heading 'Illic Jacet./In Memoriam./C. A. S.' It is unsigned.

The Edwardian is the magazine of King Edward's School, Bath. 'C. A. S.' was Lieutenant Clement Aubrey Symons, an old boy of the School and Housman's nephew, who had been killed in action. In a letter to his sister, dated 5 October 1915, on receipt of this news, Housman wrote: 'I do not know that I can do better than send you some verses that I wrote many years ago; because the essential business of poetry, as it has been said, is to harmonise the sadness of the universe, and it is somehow more sustaining and healing than prose.' It may be presumed that this prompted the *Edwardian* printing, even though its text does not follow the MS which Housman sent to his sister, the first page of which is reproduced in Plate V.

Reprinted *Last Poems* IV (see No. 5 for a note on the variations of text).

78
The Olive
(1902)

The Outlook, Vol. IX, No. 227. Saturday, 7 June 1902.

The poem is printed on p. 592, signed in full.

Reprinted *Collected Poems*, p. 240 (not from the text, but from a manuscript), as 'Additional Poems' XXIII.

79
The Parallelogram
(1904)

U.C.L. Union Magazine, Vol. 1, No. 1, Christmas Term 1904.

On pp. 21–22 is the first printing of *The Parallelogram, or Infant Optimism*. 11 four-line stanzas, unsigned.

The *Union Magazine* is the magazine of University College, London.

See No. 10 for reprint.

80
The Amphisbaena
(1906)

U.C.L. Union Magazine, Vol. 2, No. 1, June 1906.

On p. 11 is the first printing of *The Amphisbaena, or The Limits of Human Knowledge*. 42 octosyllabic couplets, unsigned.

This is entirely different from the set of untitled verses on the same subject published in the *Memoir* (p. 233), and *The Edwardian*, September 1936, p. 167 (with 6 variations).

See No. 10 for reprint.

81
The Crocodile
(1911)

U.C.L. Union Magazine, Vol. 5, No. 1, March 1911.

On p. 159 is the first printing of *The Crocodile, or Public Decency*. 46 octosyllabic couplets, unsigned.

This number of the magazine also contains, loosely inserted, a caricature representing Housman about to deliver the Foundation

Oration on Thomas Campbell, with the apprehensive shade of the poet in the background and the caption 'Mr. Thomas Campbell begins to wish he hadn't.'

See No. 10 for reprint.

82
The First of May
(1914)

The Cambridge Review, 29 April 1914.

On p. 386 is the first printing of *The First of May* ('The orchards half the way'), signed in full.

Reprinted in the *Literary Digest* (New York), Vol. XLVIII, No. 23, p. 1369, 6 June 1914; and *Last Poems* XXXIV.

83
The Conflict
(1915)

The Edwardian, Vol. VII, No. 19, December 1915.

Inserted in this number of the magazine (see also 47a) is a four-page leaflet on plate paper in memory of Housman's nephew, Lieut. C. A. Symons. On p. [2] of this leaflet, is printed 'Her strong enchantments broken' (for 'failing'), unsigned, under the title of *The Conflict*. A note states that 'the above fine lines . . . were copied by Lieutenant Symons into an autograph book', and Mrs. Symons has stated that the variation 'foot on her neck' for 'knife at her neck' in line 4 was introduced by Lieut. Symons in the process of copying. For the other textual differences see No. 5.

Set up as No. XLIII in *A Shropshire Lad*, but deleted by Housman in page-proof, dated 23 December 1895.[1]

Reprinted *Last Poems* III, untitled.

---

[1] In the collection of John Carter, now in the Lilly Library, Indiana University.

65

84
The Sage to the Young Man
(1916)

The Edwardian, Vol. 7, No. 20, April 1916.

On p. 486 is printed for the first time *The Sage to the Young Man* ('O youth whose heart is right'). It is unsigned and described as 'From an unpublished MS'.

Reprinted *More Poems* IV. Of the several differences between this and the *More Poems* text, one—*duty* in line 4 for *Virtue*—is stated by Mrs. Symons to have been a deliberate alteration by the editor of *The Edwardian*.

This poem also had been intended for publication in *A Shropshire Lad*, as No. XLII of the series, but Housman deleted it in page-proof (which survives).[1] An analysis of the development of the text, as shown in the three printed versions and five MSS versions, was published by John Carter in *The Times Literary Supplement*, 5 and 12 June 1943.

85
Verses: 'As I gird on for fighting'
(1917)

The Blunderbuss, No. 3, March 1917.

On p. 36 this poem is printed for the first time, under the title *Verses*, signed in full.

The Blunderbuss was an illustrated miscellany produced at Trinity College, Cambridge, by the 5th Officer Cadet Battalion, and printed at the University Press.

Reprinted in *The Trinity Magazine* (Cambridge), Vol. II, No. 5, p. 4, November 1920; and *Last Poems* II.

---

[1] In the collection of John Carter, now in the Lilly Library, Indiana University.

86

Epitaph on an Army of Mercenaries

(1917)

The Times, 31 October 1917.

On p. 7, under a leading article on 'The Anniversary of Ypres', is the first printing of *Epitaph on an Army of Mercenaries* ('These, in the day when heaven was falling'), signed in full.

Reprinted in the *Literary Digest* (New York), Vol. LVII, No. 7, p. 37, 18 May 1918.

This poem was released by the author to anthologists, and some of these printings (e.g. *Valour and Vision: Poems of the War 1914–1918*, edited by Jacqueline T. Trotter (London [etc.]: Longmans, Green & Co., 1920, p. 117), 1920)[1] preceded *Last Poems*, in which it was reprinted as No. XXXVII.

87

Notes on English Literature

(1921)

Cambridge University Reporter. No. 2363, Vol. LII, No. 13, Tuesday, 29 November 1921.

On p. 300, in an article entitled 'Cambridge Philological Society' is the first printing of abstracts from Housman's paper, read 17 November 1921, on emendations in Dryden, Byron, Rossetti, Stevenson, and Shelley.

The abstracts were reprinted in the *Proceedings of the Cambridge Philological Society*, Nos. CXVIII–CXX [Lent, Easter, and Michaelmas Terms, 1921], in an article entitled 'Third Meeting,' pp. 16–17 (Cambridge University Press, 1922).

The reprint only is listed in Gow, p. 79.

---

[1] The earliest appearance in a book is probably in *Fragments from Parnassus: Being Parts or the whole of Great and Good Poems*, edited by Charles L. Dana (Woodstock, Vermont: The Elm Tree Press, 1919), p. 17 (anonymous, but with a line under the title, 'Printed in the London Times, October 31, 1917').

88
The Application of Thought to Textual Criticism
(1922)

Proceedings of the Classical Association. August 1921. Vol. XVIII. London: John Murray, 1922.

Housman's paper is printed on pp. 67–84 of this red-wrappered octavo. It had been delivered at Cambridge on 4 August 1921.

Reprinted in *Selected Prose* (No. 21, above), pp. 131–150; and *The Classical Papers* (No. 26, above), Vol. 3, pp. 1058–1069.

89
The Defeated
(1939)

The Virginia Quarterly Review (University of Virginia, Charlottesville), Vol. XV, No. 4, Autumn 1939.

On p. [541] is the first printing of *The Defeated* ('In battles of no renown'), signed in full.

Reprinted in *Collected Poems*, pp. 234–235, with one variation: line 9 reads 'O soldiers . . .' instead of 'Oh, soldiers . . .'. The poem is also reprinted in *The Best Poems of 1940*, selected by Thomas Moult (London: Jonathan Cape; New York: Harcourt Brace, 1941), p. 47.

90
Sir Walter Raleigh
(1953)

Etudes Anglaises (Paris: Didier), Vol. VI, No. 4, November 1953.

On pp. 346–349 is the first printing, with Laurence Housman's permission, of A. E. Housman's earliest surviving piece of verse, composed for the Bromsgrove School English verse prize in 1873, when its author was 14 years old; it was not successful.

The MS is now in the Lilly Library, Indiana University.

91

Latin Inscriptions

(1955)

The Classical Journal. Vol. 50, No. 4, January 1955.

On pp. 159–166 are printed eight prose inscriptions in Latin by A. E. Housman: to Henry Montagu Butler, Joseph Prior, Henry Martyn Taylor, James Whitbread Lee Glaisher, Reginald Vere Laurence, for the Flaxman Gallery, the Kyteless Block (Bromsgrove School), and the Scott collection of Burmese books (University Library, Cambridge). (The Butler and Kyteless inscriptions have been previously printed.)

'Hendecasyllables,' *The Bromsgrovian*, 25 May 1882, is also reprinted here (see No. 72).

92

De Amicitia

(1967)

Encounter, Vol. XXIX, No. 4, October 1967.

On pp. 33–41 is Laurence Housman's *A. E. Housman's 'De Amicitia'*, annotated by John Carter, consisting of a 20-page article (undated) in Laurence Housman's hand, here first printed, and quotations from A. E. Housman's pocket diary for 1888 and from 14 leaves extracted by L.H. from those for 1889–1891. The material deals with Housman's relationship with Moses and Adalbert Jackson, which the cover of *Encounter* calls 'A. E. Housman's "Hidden Grief".'

An unauthorized book, *Alfred Edward Housman's 'De Amicitia'*, by Laurence Housman, reprints the texts above in a limited edition of 200 copies (London: The Little Rabbit Book Company, 1976), with quotations from *A Shropshire Lad* and *More Poems*, and without John Carter's annotations or any reference to *Encounter*.

In John Carter's 'Corrigenda & Addenda,' *Encounter*, 1968, is an unpublished letter from A. E. Housman to Miss M. A. Jackson, dated 25 May 1929 (typed copy, British Museum Add. MS. 45861).

69

93
Swinburne
(1969)

The Cornhill Magazine, No. 1061, Autumn 1969.

On pp. 380–400 is the first printing of *Swinburne* from the unsigned typescript discovered in the papers of Geoffrey Madan; it is preceded by an introductory note by John Sparrow.

The essay, with Mr. Sparrow's note, is reprinted in *The American Scholar* (Washington, D.C.), Vol. 39, No. 1, pp. 59–79, Winter 1969–70.

PERIODICALS CONTAINING ORIGINAL MATERIAL

94
Letter to a Would-Be Poet
(1928)

Notes and Queries, Vol. CLIV, No. 17, 28 April 1928.

On p. 289, in 'Memorabilia', is a letter reprinted from Messrs. Goodspeed's Catalogue of Autographs, No. 174, to a would-be poet.

Reprinted in *The Letters of A. E. Housman* (No. 24), p. 225.

95
Letter to R. A. Scott-James
(1936)

The London Mercury, Vol. XXXIV, No. 200, June 1936.

On p. 101 is letter, dated 21 April 1936, to R. A. Scott-James.

Reprinted in *The Letters of A. E. Housman* (No. 24), p. 392.

96
Postcard to Virginia Rice
(1936)

The Saturday Review of Literature (New York), Vol. XIV, No. 12, 18 July 1936.

On p. 14 is a postcard, dated 15 October 1932, to Virginia Rice.

Reprinted on the dust-wrapper of the American edition of *More Poems* (No. 13) and in *The Letters of A. E. Housman* (No. 24), p. 324.

97
Letter to Neilson Abeel
(1936)

The Forum and Century (New York), Vol. XCVI, No. 4, October 1936.

On p. 192 is a letter, dated 4 October 1935, to Neilson Abeel.

Reprinted in *The Princeton University Library Chronicle*, Vol. XIII, No. 1, Autumn 1951, pp. 18–19; and *The Letters of A. E. Housman* (No. 24), p. 377.

98
Laurence Housman's *Memories*
(1936)

John O'London's Weekly, Vol. XXXVI, Nos. 913, 914, 915, 9, 16, 23 October 1936.

Memories of A. E. Housman, by Laurence Housman, contains on pp. 38, 39 of No. 913, two light verses, 'An acorn tumbled from the oak' and 'Summer' (21 lines); on p. 112 of No. 914, a parody, 'When I was born in a world of sin' (4 lines); on p. 108 of No. 914, a letter, dated 14 March 1894, to *The Standard*; and on p. 148 of No. 915, a poem, 'Oh who is that young sinner with the handcuffs on his wrists?' (16 lines). 'Summer' is reprinted in the Bromsgrove Memorial Supplement, p. 18, and Laurence Housman's *A.E.H.* (No. 52), pp. 33–34; 'When I was born in a world of sin' in Laurence Housman's *A.E.H.*, p. 103; the letter to *The Standard* in Laurence Housman's *A.E.H.*, pp. 73–74; and in *The Letters of A. E. Housman* (No. 24), pp. 30–31; and 'Oh who is that young sinner with the handcuffs on his wrists?' in *A.E.H.*, p. 226, as 'Additional Poems' XVIII; and in *The Collected Poems* (No. 14).

See Laurence Housman's 'A Poet in the Making': *Atlantic Monthly*, Vol. 178, July 1946, pp. 116–123.

99
Letters to Geoffrey Tillotson
(1937)

English: The Magazine of the English Association, Vol.
I, No. 6, 1937.

On pp. 489–490 are excerpts from six letters, dated 23 Jan. 1935,
5 March 1935, 28 April 1935, 20 May 1935, 24 June 1935, 17 July
1935, to Geoffrey Tillotson.

They are reprinted in Geoffrey Tillotson, *Essays in Criticism and
Research* (Cambridge: At the University Press, 1942), pp. 161–162;
all except the 20 May 1935 are reprinted in full in *The Letters of A.
E. Housman* (No. 24), pp. 367, 368, 369, 372–373, 373.

100
Letter to M. Maurice Pollet
(1937)

Etudes Anglaises (Paris: Didier), 1re Année. No. V,
Septembre 1937.

On pp. 403–404 (preceded by facsimile, in part, on p. 402) is a
letter, dated 5 Feb. 1933, to M. Maurice Pollet.

Reprinted in Grant Richards, *Housman: 1897–1936* (No. 55), pp.
269–271; in John Carter and John Sparrow, *A. E. Housman: An
Annotated Hand-List*, pp. 45–47; and in *Letters of A. E. Housman*
(No. 24), pp. 328–329.

101
Marginalia in Beck and Francis Thompson
(1938)

The Colophon, New Series, Vol. III, No. 1, Winter
1938.

On p. 62 are marginalia in Beck's *Index Euripideus* and Francis
Thompson's *Poems*.

102
Letter to Sir James Barrie
(1938)

The Lancet (London), Vol. I, p. 912, 16 April 1938.

Quotes 'A Consulting Physician' (Sir Walter Langdon-Brown) on an exchange of letters between Sir James Barrie and Housman; the same exchange, with variant readings, is quoted by Sir Hugh Walpole in the *Mark Twain Quarterly*, Vol. IV, No. 4, p. 19, Summer–Fall 1941. The *Lancet* version is reprinted in Grant Richards's *Housman: 1897–1936* (No. 55), p. 385; and both in the *Bulletin of Bibliography*, Vol. 22, No. 4, p. 80, September–December 1957.

Henry Maas, *The Letters of A. E. Housman* (No. 24), p. 262n, could not substantiate the story and does not reprint the letters.

103
Letters to Grant Richards
(1941)

The Mark Twain Quarterly (Webster Groves, Missouri), Vol. IV, No. 4, Summer–Fall 1941.

On pp. 11–15, 23 are 38 letters and excerpts, dated from 24 April 1928 to 19 March 1936, to Grant Richards.

These letters and excerpts do not appear in Grant Richards's *Housman: 1897–1936* (No. 55); 15 of them are reprinted in *The Letters of A. E. Housman* (No. 24).

104
Marginalia in Blunt and Kipling
(1941)

Notes and Queries, Vol. CLXXXI, No. 22, 29 November 1941.

On p. 301 are three marginalia in W. S. Blunt's *Love Sonnets of Proteus* and Rudyard Kipling's *The Seven Seas* and *The Five Nations*.

105
Marginalia in Jevons's *Logic*
(1943)

PMLA: Publications of the Modern Language Association of America, Vol. LVIII, No. 2, June 1943.

On 584–587 are eight marginalia in W. Stanley Jevons's *Elementary Lessons in Logic . . .* (1877) and in some guidebooks.

106
Letters to Grant Richards and Others
(1943)

The Mark Twain Quarterly, Vol. V, No. 4, Spring 1943.

On pp. 11–14, 24, are 14 letters and excerpts, dated from 20 Jan. 1906 to 2 March 1934, to Blanche Bane (Mrs. William S. Kuder), F. C. Owlett, Grant Richards (4), The Windsor Press, B. F. Harz, Charles Wilson (?), and an unnamed correspondent (5).

Only one of these letters—to Grant Richards, 2 March 1934—is reprinted in *The Letters of A. E. Housman* (No. 24), p. 351.

107
Letters to J. P. Postgate and Others
(1946)

The Durham Library Journal, Vol. XXXVIII, No. 3, June 1946.

On p. 93 are three letters, dated 22 Feb. 1908, 25 July 1926, and 7 Jan. 1927, to J. B. Postgate, an unnamed correspondent, and Charles Wilson.

All are reprinted in *The Letters of A. E. Housman* (No. 24), pp. 94, 240, and 245–246; the last two in *Poet Lore* (No. 108), pp. 259–260.

108
Letters to Cyril Clemens and Others
(1947)

Poet Lore (Boston, Mass.), Vol. LIII, No. 3, Autumn 1947.

On pp. 255–262 are 17 letters, dated from 25 July 1926 to 2 March 1936, to Cyril Clemens (6), Gerald Chapman, Gerald Bullett (3), Malcolm MacLaren, Bernard Frechkman, William Hamilton, E. H. W. Meyerstein, William Johnson, Charles Wilson, and an unnamed correspondent.

Three of the letters to Cyril Clemens, those to Charles Wilson, and an unnamed correspondent are reprinted in *The Letters of A. E. Housman* (No. 24).

109
Marginalia in Galsworthy
(1948)

The Review of English Studies (Oxford), Vol. XXIV, No. 95, July 1948.

On pp. 240–241 are five marginalia in John Galsworthy's *The Man of Property* and one notation in John Masefield's 'The Daffodil Fields'.

110
Fifteen More Letters
(1950)

The Dalhousie Review (Halifax, Nova Scotia), Vol. XXIX, No. 4, January 1950.

On pp. 402–410 are 15 letters, dated from 6 Sept. 1901 to 18 February 1936, to Horatio F. Brown, The Editor of *Country Life*, Messrs Grant Richards & Co., Grant Richards (?), F. C. Owlett, a Mr. Leippert, I. R. Brussel (3), a Mr. Rubin, an unnamed correspondent, Ellis D. Robb (2), the Rev. Delos O'Brian, and P. Ayres.

Six of the letters—to Horatio F. Brown, The Editor of *Country Life*, F. C. Owlett, Mr. Leippert, I. R. Brussel, and the Rev. Delos O'Brian—are reprinted in *The Letters of A. E. Housman* (No. 24).

III
Marginalia in Cicero and Leavis
(1951)

The Papers of the Bibliographical Society of America, Vol. XLV, No. 4, Fourth Quarter 1951.

On pp. 358–359 are marginal notations in a Cicero textbook (London, 1905) and F. R. Leavis's *New Bearings in English Poetry*.

II2
Twelve Unpublished Poems
(1951)

University of Toronto Quarterly, Vol. XX, No. 3, April 1951, pp. 254–256: an unfinished narrative poem concerning 'Ned Lear', 20 lines.

College English (Chicago), Vol. XII, No. 8, May 1951, pp. 439–440: three poems of 4, 4, and 14 lines.

University of Kansas City Review, Vol. XVII, No. 2, Summer 1951, pp. 286–287: six 4-line poems.

The New York Times Book Review, 17 June 1951, p. 27: a quatrain Housman said he dreamt was from George Eliot.

The Dalhousie Review (Halifax, Nova Scotia), Vol. XXI, No. 3, Autumn 1951, pp. 196–197: a poem of beeches, 16 lines.

Most of the material, in different forms, is reprinted in Tom Burns Haber's *The Manuscript Poems of A. E. Housman* (No. 18).

113
Letter to Sir Sydney Cockerell
(1952)

The Papers of the Bibliographical Society of America, Vol. XLVI, No. 1, First Quarter 1952.

On p. 70 is a letter, dated 1 November 1922, to Sydney Cockerell.

Reprinted in Tom Burns Haber's *The Manuscript Poems of A. E. Housman* (No. 18), p. 131, and in *The Letters of A. E. Housman* (No. 24), p. 207.

114
Letter to Arthur Darby Nock
(1952)

Harvard Theological Review, Vol. XLV, No. 1, January 1952.

On p. 1 is a letter, dated 27 Jan. 1926, to Arthur Darby Nock.

Reprinted in *The Letters of A. E. Housman* (No. 24), p. 421.

115
Marginalia in R. L. Stevenson
(1956)

The American Book Collector, Vol. VII, No. 2, October 1956.

On pp. 18–20 are three marginalia in Robert Louis Stevenson's *The Master of Ballantrae: A Winter's Tale*.

116
Marginalia in Tucker, Nettleship, and Carlyle
(1957)

The American Book Collector, Vol. VII, No. 9, June 1957.

On pp. 3–5 are marginalia in T. G. Tucker's edition of *The Sonnets of Shakespeare* (Cambridge: University Press, 1924), H. Nettleship's *Key Passages for Translation into Latin Prose* (London: George Bell and Sons, 1887), and Thomas Carlyle's *Sartor Resartus: The Life and Opinions of Herr Teufelsdröckh* (London: Chapman and Hall, 1897).

117
Letter to Phillip Holmes
(1968)

Notes and Queries, Vol. CCXIII, No. 2, February 1968.

On p. 59 is a letter, dated 6 January 1934, to Phillip Holmes.

118
Letter to Paul V. Love
(1968)

The Victorian Newsletter, No. 33, Spring 1968.

On p. 48 is a letter, dated 14 Feb. 1927, to Paul V. Love.

119
Letter to Edwin Markham
(1970)

Markham Review (Staten Island, New York), Vol. 2, No. 3, May 1970.

Unpaged, contains a letter, dated 31 October 1926, to Edwin Markham, fully described but text not quoted; MS in the Kent State University (Kent, Ohio) Library.

120
Five Letters to H. P. R. Finberg
(1971)

The Times Literary Supplement, No. 3,642, 17 December 1971.

On p. 1574 are five letters, dated 1 Feb. 1929, 7 Feb. 1929, 26 May 1929, 29 July 1929, and 22 Nov. 1929, to H. P. R. Finberg, preceded by an excerpt from a letter, dated 14 July 1927, to an unnamed correspondent.

121
Letters to Sir James G. Frazer and F. M. Cornford
(1974)

Greek, Roman, and Byzantine Studies, Vol. 15, No. 4, Fall 1974.

On pp. 357–364 are four letters, dated 17 May 1913, 21 May 1913, 7 March 1915, and 22 Oct. 1927, to Sir James G. Frazer; and three letters, dated 3 May 1920, 14 Oct. 1920, and 1 May 1934, to F. M. Cornford.

122
Marginalia in Petronius
(1974)

The Classical World, Vol. LXVII, April–May 1974.

On pp. 364–365 are 10 marginalia in L. Friedlaender's edition of Petronius's *Cena Trimalchionis* (Leipzig, 1906).

123
Five Letters to I. R. Brussel
(1975)

Housman Society Journal, Vol. 2, 1975.

On pp. 17–19 are five letters, dated 30 August 1930, 30 Sept. 1930, 4 June 1931, 2 July 1931, 23 Jan. 1936 (a postcard), to I. R. Brussel.

124
Letters to A. F. Scholfield, Richards Press, and Horatio F. Brown
(1975)

Housman Society Journal, Vol. 2, 1975.

On pp. 33–35 are three letters, one (a fragment) undated, two, dated 14 May 1931 and 3 Nov. 1922, to A. F. Scholfield, the Richards Press, and Horatio F. Brown.

125
Letter to the Rev. Greville Cooke
(1977)

Housman Society Journal, Vol. 3, 1977.

On p. 20 is a letter, dated 21 Feb. 1935, to the Rev. Greville Cooke.

126
Two Letters to Geoffrey Wethered
(1978)

Housman Society Journal, Vol. 4, 1978.

On pp. 5–6 are two letters, dated 13 Sept. 1933 and 9 Dec. 1933, to Geoffrey Wethered.

A fragment of the 13 Sept. 1933 letter was published in *English Studies* (Amsterdam), Anglo-American Supplement 1969, pp. lxi–lxii.

127
Letters to John Masefield and Others
(1978)

The Journal of the Book Club of Detroit, Vol. 3, No. 1, Spring 1978.

On pp. 21–25 are three letters, dated 18 Jan. 1933, 26 Oct. 1934, and 3 June 1935, to Katharine Symons, a Miss Roberts, and John Masefield.

127A
Light Verse and Parodies
(1946)
The Atlantic Monthly, Vol. 178, No. 1, July 1946.

'A Poet in the Making', by Laurence Housman, contains, on pp. 116–123, three humorous verses ('So, when once a Countless bonny', 12 lines; 'Oh, what should I be but a turkey', 18 lines; 'And so, I wish, and long, and sigh', 4 lines); a Latin verse translation ('Black Spirits and White that mingle as they may', 4 lines); and 15 light verses and parodies, including 'Fragment of a Greek Tragedy' and 'Fragment of an English Opera', reprinted from various sources.

BOOKS AND PAMPHLETS
ABOUT A.E.H.

128
Robert Hamilton's *Housman the Poet*
(1953)

Housman the Poet. By Robert Hamilton. Exeter: Sydney Lee, 1953.

129
Ian Scott-Kilvert's *A. E. Housman*
(1955)

A. E. Housman. By Ian Scott-Kilvert. London, New York, Toronto: Published for The British Council and the National Book League by Longmans, Green & Co., 1955.

Writers and Their Work: No. 69. Reprinted, reset, with additions, 1965.

130
F. D. Sinclair's *A. E. Housman: An Evaluation*
(1957)

A. E. Housman: An Evaluation. The Text of a Lecture Delivered at the University of South Africa Vacation Schools in July, 1956. By F. D. Sinclair. Pretoria: Mededelings van die Universiteit van Suid-Afrika, Communications of the University of South Africa, 1957.

131
Otto Skutsch's *Alfred Edward Housman*
(1960)

Alfred Edward Housman 1859–1936: An Address Delivered at the Centenary Celebrations in University College London During the Third International Congress of Classical Studies. By Otto Skutsch, Dr. Phil., on 3 September 1959. [London] University of London, The Athlone Press, 1960.

Published by The Athlone Press, University of London; University of Toronto Press, Toronto; Oxford University Press, Inc., New York.

132
Christopher Ricks's *Collection of Critical Essays*
(1968)

A. E. Housman: A Collection of Critical Essays. Edited by Christopher Ricks. Englewood Cliffs, New Jersey: Prentice-Hall, Inc., 1968.

Introduction by Christopher Ricks, followed by poems by W. H. Auden, Ezra Pound, and Kingsley Amis, and essays by Edmund Wilson, John Wain, W. H. Auden, Cyril Connolly (with replies by F. L. Lucas, Martin Cooper, L. P. Wilkinson, and John Sparrow), Randall Jarrell, Cleanth Brooks, Richard Wilbur, Christopher Ricks, Morton Zauwen Zabel, F. W. Bateson, J. P. Sullivan, and John Sparrow. (All poems and essays are reprinted from other sources.)

133
B. J. Leggett's *Housman's Land of Lost Content*
(1970)

Housman's Land of Lost Content: A Critical Study of *A Shropshire Lad*. By B. J. Leggett. Knoxville: The University of Tennessee Press, 1970.

134
Yutaka Takeuchi's *Exhaustive Concordance to the Poems*
(1971)

The Exhaustive Concordance to the Poems of A. E. Housman. Edited by Yutaka Takeuchi. Tokyo: Shohakusha Publishing Company, 1971.

Basic text used is *The Collected Poems* but does not record the words of the three translations from the Greek dramatists.

135
B. J. Leggett's *The Poetic Art of A. E. Housman*
(1978)

The Poetic Art of A. E. Housman: Theory and Practice. Lincoln and London: University of Nebraska Press, 1978.

TRANSLATIONS

136
Versions from 'A Shropshire Lad'
(1929)

Versions from 'A Shropshire Lad'. By Cyril Asquith. Oxford: Basil Blackwell, MCMXXIX.

190 × 140 mm. 16 leaves. Tan wrappers, printed in black.

Translation into Latin of 12 lyrics from *A Shropshire Lad*, with the English on opposite pages: VI, XI, XII, XIII, XV, XVIII, XL, XLIX, XLVI, XLVII, LVII, LXIII.

137
Housman's Introductory Lecture
(1938)

Housman's Introductory Lecture, 1892 (pp. 32–39). Translated into Greek. By Vincent Turner, S. J. Campion Hall. Oxford: Basil Blackwell, 1938.

236 × 158 mm. 10 leaves. Cream wrappers, stitched, printed in black. Cover reads: Gaisford Prize Composition: Greek Prose, 1938.

Translation into Greek, with the English on opposite pages.

138
Digte
(1944)

A. E. Housman. Digte. Ved Poul P. M. Pedersen, Forord af C. A. Bodelsen. København: Aschehoug Dansk Forlag (Indehaver: G. M. Steffensen), MCMXLIV.

232 × 168 mm. 28 leaves. Blue wrappers, printed in white (front cover), and black (spine and back cover).

Translation into Danish of 24 lyrics from *A Shropshire Lad* and *Last Poems*.

139
Nombre y Naturaleza de la Poesía
(1945)

A. E. Housman. De la Universidad de Cambridge. Nombre y Naturaleza de la Poesía. Traducción por Octavio G. Barreda. Libros del Hijo Pródigo. Ediciones Letras de Mexico, [1945].

155 × 105 mm. 38 leaves. Maroon cloth. Lettered in gilt on spine.

Of this translation into Spanish of *The Name and Nature of Poetry*, 45 numbered copies were for members of the Club del Bibliófilo Mexicano, and five on special paper (I to V) for the author.

The text follows the American edition, in which there is an error (on p. 62) in a quotation from Shakespeare that was never corrected.

140
Rolando Anzilotti's *La Poesia di A. E. Housman*
(1958)

La Poesia di A. E. Housman. Di Rolando Anzilotti, Libreria Editrice Florentina. Pistoia: Tipografia Pistoiese, 1958.

Pp. 101–150 contain 'Il Name e la Natura della Poesia,' Leslie Stephen Lecture, Tenuta a Cambridge il 9 Maggio 1933, a translation into Italian of *The Name and Nature of Poetry*.

The text follows the first English edition, containing the error (on pp. 140–141) in a quotation from Shakespeare.

[References are to item numbers, not pages]